Time and Then Some
Literature-Based Thematic Activities

Veronika Winkler • **Joan Preston** • **Diane Chait**

Thinking Publications
Eau Claire, Wisconsin

06 05 04 03 02 01 00 99 98   10 9 8 7 6 5 4 3 2 1

Library of Congress Cataloging-in-Publication Data

Winkler, Veronika.

    Literature-based thematic activities. Time and then some / Veronika Winkler, Joan Preston, Diane Chait.

       p. cm.

    Includes bibliographical references.

    ISBN 1-888222-19-0 (pbk.)

    1. Language arts (Early childhood) 2. Literature—Study and teaching (Early childhood) 3. Time—Study and teaching (Early childhood) 4. Early childhood education—Activity programs. I. Preston, Joan. II. Chait, Diane. III. Title.

LB1139.5.L35W57 1998

372.6—dc21

98-11853

CIP

Illustrations drawn under contract by Terry Medaris and Kris Gausman

Cover design by Kris Gausman

Printed in the United States of America

**THINKING
PUBLICATIONS**
A Division of McKinley Companies, Inc.

424 Galloway Street • Eau Claire, WI 54703
1-800-225-GROW(4769) • FAX 1-800-828-8885
E-Mail: custserv@ThinkingPublications.com
www.ThinkingPublications.com

Dedication

To our husbands, Art, Dick, and Howard,

for their encouragement and patience

Table of Contents

Preface

We invite you to join an educational expedition in active learning. Explore and discover the excitement of teaching communication skills—listening, speaking, reading, and writing—in a child-centered, collaborative environment.

We thank our colleagues in Manalapan-Englishtown Regional Schools for their support and encouragement while we developed *Literature-Based Thematic Activities*. A special thanks to our typist, Kathy Sauer, who worked with zeal to help create the original prototype. Last, but most of all, we wish to thank our families, who showed faith in our abilities, urged us to go on when we became discouraged, and joined us in celebrating our accomplishments.

About the Authors

Veronika Winkler is a principal in the Bridgewater-Raritan School District. Previously she worked as language arts supervisor for the Manalapan-Englishtown Regional Schools, Englishtown, New Jersey. She received a B.S. degree in education from Syracuse University, and an M.Ed. degree from Trenton State College, New Jersey. She has presented to early childhood educators at the local, state, and national levels. She served as secretary to the New Jersey Association for Supervision and Curriculum Development.

Joan Preston currently volunteers and substitutes in the MSAD #15 Schools in Gray, Maine after working as a whole language and manipulative math consultant and after 30 years of teaching at the primary level in the Manalapan-Englishtown Regional Schools. She received a B.S. degree in Elementary Education from Trenton State College (New Jersey) and is certified in Early Childhood Education.

Diane Chait teaches first grade at Belmont Day School in Belmont, Massachusetts. She received a B.A. degree from Grinnell College, a M.S. degree in curriculum and instruction from the University of Wisconsin, and a certificate as a reading specialist from Pennsylvania State University. Since 1971, she has taught grades 1 through 6 as well as in the Chapter One Program. She has made presentations and conducted workshops on reading and language arts.

Introduction

The *Literature-Based Thematic Activities* series demonstrates how thematic units and literature can develop communication and literacy skills, integrate curriculum content, and provide structure for learning activities. The series illustrates how using a broad theme captures children's interests and focuses their learning. The series also recognizes that reading, writing, speaking, and listening develop in conjunction with one another rather than in a sequence (e.g., children talk while they create art, tell stories while they play, use letters when they talk and write). The series is intended for children in preschool, kindergarten, and first grade and is especially amenable for—but not limited to—collaborative teaching in an inclusive setting.

Threaded throughout the books in this series are standard activities that

- promote the acquisition of communication and literacy skills—speaking, listening, reading, and writing;
- create an appreciation for literature and the authoring process;
- develop communication skills through real-life activities;
- use technology;
- provide experiences that employ the scientific method;
- employ the mathematics standards recommended by the National Council of Mathematics Teachers; and
- support the understanding and appreciation of cultural and personal differences that occur in our society.

In addition, ideas are included for room organization, example discussions, and child-centered activities to help children make appropriate connections among the

disciplines in the preschool and early elementary classrooms. Sample checklists and other methods for evaluating child progress are also included (see Appendix A).

Literature-Based Thematic Activities incorporates many of the traditionally taught concepts into new and exciting thematic units. *Time and Then Some*—the second in the series of *Literature-Based Thematic Activities*—includes suggestions for using a time theme. Time is a difficult concept for youngsters to grasp and is a concept every preschool and primary classroom addresses.

In this resource, children learn about time as an interval; they discuss and explore time as a way to describe *how long* something will take. They also study time as a way to tell *when* something will take place. They read or listen to trade books that explore concepts of time (e.g., before, after, week, month, year, yesterday, tomorrow). (See pages 9–10 for a discussion of subtheme units.)

Target Users

Literature-Based Thematic Activities is especially effective in inclusionary preschool, kindergarten, and grade 1 classrooms. These settings might include children of various levels with numerous special needs. In an inclusionary classroom, educators teach collaboratively. In addition to the preschool or elementary classroom teacher, the collaboration may include a speech-language pathologist, learning disabilities teacher, early childhood teacher, or reading specialist who can also easily implement the activities described in this resource.

Strategies to Support the Inclusionary Model

All students benefit from a language-rich program; this includes students with language and learning disorders or students who are learning English as a second language. *Literature-Based Thematic Activities* accommodate children of various backgrounds, abilities, and interests using the following strategies.

1. *Student-generated activities*—Because so many of the materials, activities, and discussions are generated by the students, individual differences are not only accepted but applauded.

2. *Sharing*—In the context of social situations such as the sharing group discussions and shared reading and writing experiences, children are encouraged to talk about themselves, express their opinions, and share their experiences.

3. *Open-ended activities*—A deliberate effort has been made to offer many open-ended activities to allow students of varying abilities and backgrounds to work together toward a common goal.

4. *Two-way learning*—Since a thematic approach is not textbook based, the learning becomes more spontaneous and individualized. "At times, the educator directs, often by structuring experiences and the environment; at other times, children direct the curriculum. It is like a ballet between a sensitive adult and the children. Both are in control, both initiate, both respond, and both take cues from one another" (Seefeldt, 1988, p. 60). Educators can create curriculum experiences that offer students academic challenges as well as provide for individual differences (Elkind, 1986). Through this two-way communication, children soon realize they can manipulate the learning process to fit their interests. With practice, the educator begins to realize how to blend children's interests with the goals and objectives of the curriculum. Because of the two-way communication, children soon realize

   • the educator values their contributions;

   • their contributions are respected by their peers;

   • their ideas form the basis of many lessons; and

   • they are responsible in part for their own learning.

5. *Scaffolding*—Learning is enhanced when the educator provides children with assistance to perform a task that ordinarily they could not complete independently (Bruner, 1975; Staton, 1984; Vygotsky, 1978). *Scaffolding* is the support provided to help learners bridge the gap between what they know and can do and the intended goal (Graves, Graves, and Braaten, 1996). It is the cueing, coaching, questioning, corroboration, and provision of information needed to help students complete a task before they are able to do it independently (Pearson, 1996). For example, in shared reading sessions, the educator not only models fluent reading but invites children to read along. This invitation allows students to successfully act as readers at an emergent stage of development. Naturally and gradually, children begin to incorporate the many skills necessary to become independent readers.

   Scaffolding has been described as one of the most effective instructional techniques available (Cazden, 1992; Rosenshine and Meister, 1992; Sweet, 1993) and is particularly useful in inclusionary settings (Graves, Graves, and Braaten, 1996). A scaffolding technique is apparent throughout this resource.

6. *Literacy experiences*—The activities assume that *all* students will benefit from literacy activities. Children are immersed in common literacy experiences designed to create a community of readers and writers. Literacy strategies support communication development for all students and do not depend on ability grouping for delivery.

Background
Emergent Literacy

Literacy is the mastery of language—in all forms including spoken, augmented, and written—that enables an individual to use language fluently for a variety of purposes (Montgomery, 1996). Literacy goes beyond learning to read, write, and spell (Mirenda, 1993). It includes learning to enjoy books, being read to, hearing stories, and becoming aware of the new knowledge a literary experience can provide. Learning to read and write begins with a young child's first experiences with print materials and books (typically book exploration begins at age 1). Children travel the literacy continuum through active engagement with written materials and with the helpful mediation of family members, teachers, and other adults (e.g., "Look at what your birthday card says!") (Montgomery, 1996).

Literature-Based Thematic Activities is replete with literary experiences for the "emergent" literacy learner (i.e., preschool-age children through grade 1). Children are exposed to literature with predictable and repetitive text designed to support the beginning reader/writer. Suggested shared reading/writing experiences follow a general pattern in which students are invited to predict, read along, reread, and respond both orally and in written form to the literature. A variety of literacy strategies are included:

- telling and retelling of events;
- graphic organizers such as comparison charting (Venn diagrams, extension charts), webbing, story maps;
- use of activity boards;
- scaffolding;
- reading selections aloud;
- singing and chanting of rhyme;
- writing before, along with, and after reading;
- journal writing and child-authored stories; and
- creative dramatizing.

Thematic Teaching

Employing thematic units to teach basic skills permits the conditions for the natural acquisition of language, as described by Cambourne and Turbill (1987), to optimally function in the classroom. In thematic-based instruction, children are surrounded by authentic literary events that require speaking, reading, and writing about subjects and topics of their interests related to a broad theme (Harste, Short, and Burke, 1988; Holdaway, 1979).

A thematic approach offers young children knowledge and experiences that they can value and actively engages students in the process of learning. Through the use of discussions and activities, children reflect on their experiences and see themselves in relation to the unit.

Thematic units teach skills through integrated content studies. Social studies, science, mathematics, and fine arts experiences are integrated with literary events. Speaking, listening, reading, and writing are the tools children use to learn about content.

Using a thematic approach to teach basic skills through content provides an opportunity to create an intellectually stimulating and language-rich environment. Children appreciate and discover the excitement of learning. Themes help to do the following:

- link all classroom activities;

- integrate subjects and learning;

- allow students with different abilities to work cooperatively on a variety of projects;

- capture children's interests;

- involve students in planning; and

- provide a structure for student exploration, the use of language, and the acquisition of basic knowledge.

Providing multiple forms of self-expression within a framework of a theme develops the relationships among listening, speaking, reading, and writing. Dramatic arts, music activities, cooking experiences, art activities, science and social studies projects, hands-on math problems, and children's literature provide youth with a rich experiential background that stimulates them to read and write. This approach takes advantage of children's prior knowledge and accommodates individual diversity. Bruner (1975), Holdaway (1979), and Strickland and Morrow (1989) are among those whose writings emphasize using the thematic-unit approach to develop a climate that actively engages students in meaningful and relevant activities. These activities require the purposeful use of language, integrate

curriculum, and provide structured learning experiences. A thematic-unit approach "provides a focal point for inquiry, for the use of language, and for cognitive development. It involves students in planning and gives them choices of authentic relevant activities within productive studies" (Goodman, 1986, p. 31).

Child-Centered Activities

Learning and teaching are far more stimulating, relevant, and spontaneous when educators bring the child's world into the teaching environment. In a child-centered environment, children are active participants who are encouraged to explore concepts based on their needs and interests, to make contributions, to help direct lessons, and to make choices. When students are given ownership, they are more likely to focus on their efforts and gain meaning from their learning experiences (Calkins, 1986; Harste, Short, and Burke, 1988; Thais, 1986).

Literature-Based Thematic Activities supports a child-centered classroom philosophy. Children share in planning activities and are given opportunities to initiate, self-direct, and assume some responsibilities for their own learning. In this active-learning environment, children are invited to participate in a variety of activities that have been modeled and demonstrated to them on many occasions by their peers and an educator, knowing that all contributions and work will be respected and valued.

Experientially Based Curriculum

An experientially based curriculum offers many opportunities to solve real problems through exploration, inventions, and play. It is best suited to teach young children the basic skills of reading, writing, and math. Experts such as Dewey (1897), Piaget and Inhelder (1969), and Goodman (1986) agree that primary school children learn best by interacting with people, by working with concrete objects, and by internalizing personal experiences. In simple terms, children learn best by doing. Giving children the time to share and communicate, to act as models for each other, and to appreciate each other's work is part of the learning environment endorsed by David Elkind. "Young children in a sound program of early childhood education have the support of activities suited to their learning styles. This eliminates the stresses occasioned by the curriculum and stilted teacher/student interaction inherent in formal instruction of highly academic programs" (Elkind, 1986, p. 635). An experientially based program utilizes child-centered activities to develop cognitive, affective, and psychomotor skills. Children also learn literacy through active engagement (Montgomery, 1996). This educational philosophy becomes evident when children work independently in activity centers, when learning through concrete experiences, and by demonstrating initiative in the learning process.

According to Katz (1987), learning environments should be intellectually oriented so children can interact in small groups and work together on a variety of interesting projects that strengthen their curiosity and desire to learn. Children should be exposed to a variety of skills, concepts, and stimulating problems initiated by the educator. They should spend considerable time in activity centers designed to promote understanding through personal experience and develop and practice their skills in situations that are purposeful, such as reading from real books, writing letters, or authoring books.

Using *Literature-Based Thematic Activities*

Blending the thematic approach with traditional kindergarten and first grade curriculum is possible. *Literature-Based Thematic Activities* integrates speaking, listening, reading, and writing experiences with the content of science, social studies, mathematics, and fine arts. There are many ways to incorporate the thematic-unit approach within the school day:

- use it to supplement an existing language arts program;
- use it to enhance the social studies/science curriculum;
- use it as a model for integrating strategies in the classroom; or
- select interesting ideas, strategies, and suggestions presented throughout this resource.

The following sample schedule shows how a typical day could be organized. If one plans to use themes in a collaborative way, the schedule should also consider collaborators' schedules.

Opening Activities

Sharing, Shared Reading/Writing Experiences (whole group)

Learning Centers (small groups)

Snack, Recess

Special Subjects/Lunch

Read-Aloud Selection

If users are not integrating themes throughout the day, *Literature-Based Thematic Activities* can still be used to teach time concepts in a more traditional way.

Organizing the Setting

An active learning environment provides children with the time and space to act on concepts, ideas, and basic skills developed by the educator. If possible, arrange the

room to accommodate large-group and small-group instruction so that children can work as a whole group, independently, or in small groups practicing and sharing ideas with their peers. Divide the space into distinct sections to include learning centers, a reading corner, and one large open space. Existing furniture can be used in creative ways. If you do not have an art table, cluster students' desks and cover them with a plastic cloth. Remember that children like to work on the floor, too. Make sure that ample space is provided for the children's materials (paper, pencils, tape, scissors, and staplers).

Creating a Print-Rich, Language-Rich Environment

In a print-rich, language-rich environment, students are surrounded by a great number of examples and models of reading and writing. To accomplish immersion, the environment invites children to listen, speak, read, and write. If using desks, they can be clustered in small groups to encourage communication. Bulletin boards can be covered with examples of students' art, writing, poetry, and experience charts filled with students' questions and responses. Shelves should be stocked with a wide variety of books, assorted paper, pencils, and supplies that are accessible to students. A cozy library/ media center with a small table, comfortable chairs, and pillows motivates children to read and talk about books. Videocassettes, tape recorders, and computers ideally should be accessible to students.

Planning with Children

Take the time to talk about the importance of helping each other, of sharing equipment, and of responsibilities for maintaining the room. This conversation may need to take place on several occasions. Role-playing is an excellent tool for initiating discussions. Have children act out how it feels when someone interferes with their play or when their work is tampered with or destroyed. Reinforce appropriate behavior when children have resolved a problem independently or appropriately. Be sure to praise them publicly. Even with the best management and organization, confrontations between children, inefficient use of time and materials, and accidents and spills will occur. Consider these interruptions as learning opportunities. Work together with the children to resolve these problems by discussing them openly and involving the children in the decision-making process. At times it will be necessary to review the rules, and sometimes it may be necessary to revise them.

Children make significant contributions to the classroom by

- sharing experiences, observations, ideas, and written work;

- supplying materials;

- working cooperatively in small groups;

- planning activities; and

- helping to organize and maintain the classroom.

Allow children to choose activities and learning centers during appropriate times of the day. A stimulating classroom environment provides children with many opportunities to make choices and decisions based on their interests and abilities. Providing children with the freedom to make choices and decisions conveys a sense of trust and confidence in their desire to learn and offers them a sense of ownership in the process. Allow children to choose the activity or the learning center they want, as long as they use the materials in each center responsibly.

Literature-Based Thematic Activities: Time and Then Some Subthemes

Literature-Based Thematic Activities: Time and Then Some includes four subtheme units:

1. Sunrise to Sunset: What Do I Do Every Day?

2. Marvelous Monday: What Do I Do Weekly?

3. Full Moon: When Is My Birthday?

4. Good Times: What Are My Favorite Days?

Time is one of the harder concepts for young children to grasp. *Time and Then Some* is designed to make this difficult topic accessible. This text sets the stage for a four- to six-week study about time.

As children learn the basic concepts dealing with time, they realize that there are different ways to think about time. They learn that time is an interval or a duration that tells how long something takes, and that time also tells when something will take place. Both concepts are explored and developed in this unit.

Each subtheme unit begins by having children think and talk about their personal experiences as they relate to time. The content of time provides many opportunities to integrate reading, writing, listening, and speaking experiences with science and social studies. A wide variety of read-aloud selections offers additional opportunities for children to explore, discuss, and learn about the concepts relating to time. Throughout the subtheme units, children are led to ask questions about how time functions. Trade books, such as *Jesse Bear, What Will You Wear?* (1986) by Nancy White Carlstrom, *Cookie's Week* (1988) by Cindy Ward, *Benjamin's 365 Birthdays* (1992) by Judi Barrett, and *How Much Is a Million?* (1994) by David Schwartz, provide background information

for understanding time. Making water clocks and planning a Good Time Parade are learning activities that provide many exciting and relevant simulations for employing concepts about time.

The exploration of time begins with the child's day. The units then progress to looking at the week, the month, and finally the year.

Each subtheme includes the following components:

1. an overview;

2. suggestions for using sharing as a springboard activity to reading and writing activities;

3. ideas for shared reading/writing experiences to teach communication and literacy skills, including developing and using class books and child-authored books, and suggestions for books to read aloud;

4. ideas for songs, movement activities, and/or games;

5. suggestions for learning centers; and

6. offerings for a related cooking experience.

The following sections explain each of these components.

Overview

The overview provides a summary of the subtheme goal. Skills and concepts developed in the subtheme unit are listed. A list of preparatory steps are described in the *Planning Ahead* section of the overview. In the *Planning Ahead* section, specific supplies needed for subtheme activities are listed, although many are typical classroom supplies. The specific games and books needed to implement activities are listed, although users should also refer to the *Alternate Read-Aloud* selections included at the end of the *Shared Reading/Writing Experience* for additional book ideas.

Finally, any activity sheets that need duplication are listed in *Planning Ahead*. The number to duplicate is dependent on the size of the group.

Sharing: From Invitations to Celebrations

This component is so named because sharing is a critical component of the learning environment. When the educator and students share knowledge, listen to each other, and encourage risk taking, they are delivering informal invitations to learn from each other. Educators and students model their thinking, interests, and work, motivating one another to do the same. For instance, an adult who reads a book and then excitedly talks about it is issuing an invitation to someone else to read that book.

Celebrating the children's successes is also an important part of the sharing component. If a 6-year-old reads a book he wrote in the writing center, and his work and success are celebrated by the group, he becomes a model for his classmates.

During sharing time, children are encouraged to talk about and share their personal experiences. This sharing time precedes reading/writing experiences and is a springboard activity designed to

- determine prior knowledge;

- maximize active participation;

- talk about and create a purpose for investigation;

- introduce vocabulary;

- establish relevance for study; and

- provide a time to share common experiences.

For these initiating activities to be successful, it is crucial for the educator to listen to and record the children's words, ideas, and thoughts. The more children are encouraged to talk about their personal experiences and to ask questions, the more excited they will become to read and write about the topics.

Lists, sentences, and questions are developed through this directed discussion in sharing time. These pave the way for subsequent shared reading/writing experiences. The experience charts generated from these discussions should be read and reread and added to as children's curiosities, comments, and backgrounds are revealed. Throughout the subtheme unit, children's attention should be redirected to these original charts to expand, direct, and nurture their investigations.

Throughout this resource, strategies that promote sharing are suggested. These are the celebrations that occur day by day. In addition, the last subtheme unit suggests a culminating community celebration—in this case, a class parade—which the children help to plan, organize, and present.

Shared Reading/Writing Experiences

The reading and writing processes are significantly enhanced when students have the opportunity to interact with the same text many times. In this resource, reading and writing skills are continually being modeled and demonstrated.

Shared Reading Experience

Shared reading experiences involve the educator and the whole class reading and rereading books, rhymes, songs, stories, poetry, class books, and language experience charts. At other times, students in small groups joined by the educator share literature

for guided reading. Many of the suggested reading materials offer rhyme, rhythm, and repetition. For younger children, shared reading experiences are designed to imitate the mood and intimate feelings of a bedtime story. For older and more skilled students, shared reading experiences form the foundation of literature groups.

Shared reading experiences should begin with students gathered close to the educator. Remember, the experiences should include warm-up activities such as discussions, poems, chants, and predicting exercises. Students should be asked to name the author and title, and tell what they think the literature is about. When appropriate, children could be asked if they recall other stories or poems by the same author. The educator may elect to record students' responses. In some instances, a close examination of pictures and their interpretation might be desirable and beneficial before reading.

Poems, rhymes, stories, and chants (related to the theme) should be read primarily for enjoyment. Clarification of content, book talk, and feelings about the literature ideally should follow each reading. Shared reading experiences are ongoing demonstrations of the reading process as children observe the adult turning the pages, reading from left to right, making meaning from the written word, and enjoying interaction with the written word. Although the suggested activities in each subtheme unit require specific book titles, an alternate list of books to read aloud is included at the end of the *Shared Reading/Writing Experience* section. These books center around the theme of time and can be read aloud to children or made available for browsing in learning centers.

Reading and rereading again and again leads to increased participation by the children. Each rereading is built upon what was read, discussed, and understood in the previous reading. Children can read along on selected phrases or whole pages. Students should not be coerced into reading along. As they hear and see the text repeatedly and when they are ready, they will take the risk of reading voluntarily. Each reading should be an enjoyable, stress-free experience.

As long as the children's interest is sustained, multiple rereading offers many opportunities to illustrate specific skills in the context of meaningful and well-known texts. Demonstrate only one or two skills at any time. Suggested activities that follow shared reading sessions, such as text matching, story mapping, and Venn diagrams, are designed to reinforce skill development without the use of worksheets and workbooks. Resist the temptation to overteach. Children should be engaged in many authentic reading and writing activities that incorporate a wide range of language skills.

In summary, shared reading experiences allow the educator to

- demonstrate the reading/writing process;

- teach specific communication skills;

- use text as a model for writing experiences;

- involve children in the reading/writing process without fear of failure; and

- create a community of readers.

Shared Writing Experience

As with shared reading experiences, shared writing experiences involve the educator and the students in talking, writing, and sharing. Students need time to think, write, rewrite, and share their work in an atmosphere that is free, relaxed, and encouraging.

Writing occurs in the whole-group situation as well as on an individual basis. Dictated lists, class books, class newspapers, and innovations of known text are the main source of whole-group demonstrations; while journals, reading logs, and child-authored works are the products of individual efforts.

In writing, children's first attempts may be scribbles, pictures, letter strings, and random words. Slowly, children will begin to use initial and final consonants to represent words. Children may temporarily "invent" spellings by using their knowledge of sound/symbol relationships and print conventions to write plausible spellings of words they have yet to learn (Lombardino, Bedford, Fortier, Carter, and Brandi, 1997). Accepting these approximations validates their attempts and spurs them to continue writing. This temporary spelling leads to the use of more expressive language because young writers can use any word that is part of their oral language. Writing experiences are also tied to demonstrations that come from real books and the group dictation process. Additionally, mini-lessons provide students with specific communication skills.

Shared writing experiences allow the educator to

- teach skills as the need arises (both individual and group);

- demonstrate the need for use of writing conventions;

- demonstrate writing for different purposes;

- illustrate connections between reading and writing; and

- encourage the collaborative process among students.

Literacy skills are taught through demonstrations in reading and writing. Many of the activities direct the educator to take dictation by recording children's thoughts and experiences on large chart paper (known as experience charts). This allows the educator to model correct spelling, phonics, letter formation, sentence structure, and punctuation to the whole group. The educator should take advantage of these opportunities by verbalizing the thoughts and actions involved in the process (e.g., saying, "I need an s sound here," "I need to start with a capital letter," or "I need help spelling this word").

These statements call attention to the process of writing. These daily demonstrations are models for reading and writing. Group dictation should be read and reread many times just like any other shared reading experience. Dictated class lists, stories, and other experience charts should be displayed around the room, so the children can use them as a resource for basic sight words, punctuation, and capitalization.

Creating Class Books

One rewarding product that can be created based on children's dictation is a class book. Creating class books can be one of the most exciting writing events for educators and students. During these cooperative writing situations, the educator can demonstrate and model an endless array of reading and writing skills. Children quickly learn that what they think and say can be written and read by others. They realize that their thoughts and words are valued enough to be recorded.

Any group event, such as cooking experiences, field trips, and unexpected happenings, can be the inspiration for this writing experience. Table 1 provides additional suggestions. Students should discuss the experience and their ideas for presenting it before dictating the class book. They can explore and raise issues about writing. After discussing a particular event, the students are invited to suggest or tell what they want the educator to write on large chart paper. To create the books, record accurately what each child says, and then read the sentence while inviting the children to read along. Occasionally, stop to point out a skill or sight word (without belaboring the point and while maintaining a lively pace). After each contribution, reread the entire piece to enhance comprehension and to spark other ideas. When children tire, lose interest, or decide to end, dictation stops.

After the story is finished, show students how to divide the story into parts for a book. Then cut the chart paper with the story into sections. If age-appropriate, have student volunteers carefully copy by writing these sections into a blank book. Have students illustrate the class book. Suggestions for formatting the book and uses for the class book are also provided in Table 1. The completed book can be read again and again as a shared reading experience.

As with anything else, the class books will improve with experience. Plan group dictation sessions routinely. In the beginning, the children's attention will be limited— and so will their stories. However, if the writing process is not laborious and the children get appropriate feedback about their first attempts, their desire to write more class books will grow along with their knowledge about language. In fact, they may beg to write class books.

Table 1

Class Books • Child-Authored Books

Topics	Suggestions for Formatting	Uses for
1. Current events in the news (e.g., space shuttle)	1. Vary books by size (e.g., small and large).	1. Place the book in a class library with a borrowing card attached.
2. Special events in school (e.g., art show)	2. Vary type of paper used for books (e.g., lined or unlined).	2. Use the book to demonstrate a specific skill.
3. Science experiments (e.g., plant journals)	3. Vary book shapes (e.g., animal and flower shapes).	3. Publish the book.
4. Social study topics (e.g., famous person)	4. Vary type of illustrations (e.g., painted, created with markers, crayons).	4. Share books in large-group and small-group settings.
5. Field trips (e.g., zoo)		5. Send books home to be read and reread.
6. Autobiographies (e.g., pets, family members, vacation)	5. Vary form, create a scrapbook (e.g., photos, colors, field trips).	6. Read books to students in other classes and other grades.
7. Cooking experiences (e.g., steps for making applesauce)	6. Hang a big notebook at the easel (e.g., to enter daily special events, individual comments).	7. Submit the class book to a children's magazine for publication.
8. Improvisations on known literature (e.g., story about Cinderfella vs. Cinderella)	7. Include a table of contents and title page.	8. Keep a collection of previous years' books for browsing.
9. Unexpected events at school (e.g., gerbil escapes)	8. Include a dedication page.	9. Keep books in the reading and writing centers for inspiration.
10. Special events in the community (e.g., local festival)	9. Vary form, keep a journal and a learning log.	

Child-Authored Books

When children have had several experiences creating class books, they will want to work in small groups, in pairs, or alone to author books. Spelling, phonics, and listening skills are developed as children use them to read and write. While children are actively involved in reading and writing their own books, the educator should offer guidance and suggestions based on individual needs and questions. Basic skill instruction is meaningful and relevant when addressing children's needs as they try to use the skills. For example, word boundaries and spacing become important to children when they realize that without them they cannot read their own writing.

Throughout the day and week, the educator should hold conferences with individual children, providing them with the skills that are developmentally appropriate. The learning will not necessarily follow the scope and sequence found in basal readers and textbooks. One child may understand and use capitalization but forget to use punctuation. Another child may use punctuation but not capitalize appropriately. Both children will acquire those skills but not in the same order or at the same time. The important thing is that children have many opportunities to learn about language through actual writing and reading experiences.

Young children will take the risks inherent in their first attempts to write and read if they feel secure and know their work will be accepted. The educator needs to encourage these first attempts with praise. As children become more confident, they will become more aware of appropriate language usage and will want to write more and more.

Like the class book, the topics and the format of the child-authored book can vary (see Table 1 on page 15). Stock many blank books of various sizes and shapes for students' use. The child-authored books should be read to the whole class before being put into a class library. Library cards and pockets can be put in each new book. Students will enjoy reading and rereading their own books and the books of others.

Songs, Movement, and Games

Each subtheme unit in *Time and Then Some* suggests songs, movement activities, and/or commercially provided games that reinforce the time theme. Songs can be sung as a group and shared with the music teacher and/or they can be tape-recorded and placed in the reading center for listening. Games can also be placed in an appropriate learning center.

Learning Centers

Each subtheme unit describes ideas for organizing learning centers. Centers provide the educator with an effective, economical, and practical method for individualizing

instruction and making learning more relevant and meaningful. Structured centers are important because they

- provide opportunities for exploring a multitude of hands-on activities;
- provide experiences that reinforce skills in all disciplines;
- promote exploration and discovery;
- allow additional time for children to apply and enrich concepts taught;
- stimulate the sharing of ideas and initiate pride in one's accomplishments;
- encourage the development of independent work habits;
- require the application of acceptable social skills and self-discipline;
- promote creativity and problem solving while developing appropriate language usage;
- offer experiences in using writing skills and recordkeeping;
- teach children to organize and handle materials in an appropriate manner; and
- offer opportunities to exchange ideas with peers.

Children should be allowed to choose the learning center they would like to participate in. When the children are allowed to choose the center and/or the project they wish to complete, individual learning rates, interests, and abilities are accommodated.

It is not necessary for every child to complete every project or activity offered in the learning centers. Each learning center contributes to a child's growth. The child who chooses the writing center over the drama center is learning and is choosing a creative response that is appropriate to that child's developmental level. Each child's experience will help develop the concepts and content of the theme, particularly if all children have an equal opportunity to share their work with their classmates.

If children are not accustomed to working independently or cooperatively in small groups, introduce the learning centers gradually. On the first day, introduce two centers, such as the art center and the reading center. Discuss the necessary equipment, organization, maintenance, and rules for each center. Ask students to help shape each center by bringing things from home such as crates for storage, scrap materials for art projects, books, games, assorted writing materials, pens and pencils, and markers; thus, creating a sense of ownership and interest in each center. Have students make signs and labels for the centers.

Begin operating these two centers for short periods of time (20 minutes). Divide the class into thirds. Assign one group to draw or read at a table while another group works at the art center and the third group works in the reading center. Rotate the

groups through each center, stopping between rotations to talk about rules and reinforce behavior. In the beginning, centers will be crowded because the other centers are not yet functioning.

In addition, the following tips will help manage the centers in a easy manner:

1. Keep pans or boxes in each center for unfinished work and work to be checked.

2. Provide a board that lists the various centers. Under each center name, screw in a number of hooks, indicating the number of children permitted in the center at one time. Each day, children select two centers where they would like to work. They hang their nametags on the hooks under the names of the centers they wish to attend.

3. Have children go to their first chosen center and remain there to work and play, stopping only when a signal (a bell or whistle) is given. At that point, children should clean up and move on to the next center. A quick check before the children move on ensures good habits.

4. Move from center to center asking questions, giving suggestions, posing problems, and providing encouragement.

5. Demonstrate any game, project, or equipment before putting it into a center.

6. Establish rules and consequences for not following the rules for each center.

7. Establish a signal system for getting children to stop, look, and listen. During the first few days, practice using the signal many times until children respond quickly and easily.

8. Expect busy noise. Occasionally it may be necessary to discuss appropriate noise level.

9. Anticipate children's disputes, messes, and other interruptions. When they occur, review each situation with the children involved and with the whole class.

As children appear ready (that is, when they understand the rules), introduce a new center. Activities in each subtheme unit are offered for seven centers (drama, writing, reading, math, art, discovery, and sand and water). Choose only those centers that seem appropriate for your classroom. However, it is recommended that at least four centers be made available. The following sections describe the rationale for each center and basic supplies to have available.

Drama Center

Dramatization allows the children to role-play and express the concepts they have learned in the various curriculum areas. This center encourages creativity, oral language, and a sharing of ideas.

Basic Supplies

puppet stage   puppets

paper   pencils

dress-up clothes

cassette player/recorder, blank tapes

props related to stories

Writing Center

The writing center invites children to write stories and books, to record events, and to create poetry that is inspired by the unit themes or personal experiences.

Basic Supplies

print sets

typewriter or computer

crayons   markers, pencils

glue or glue sticks   scissors

magazines   newspapers

alphabet chart   word lists

blank books for child-authoring

a variety of paper (lined and unlined), note paper, Post-It note pads

dictionary and/or picture dictionary

Reading Center

In this center, children can revisit the literature explored during shared reading/ writing experiences. Children can listen to favorite stories and poems, recorded commercially or by the educator. Children can read along as they listen. They also can record their own stories or reading.

Basic Supplies

table and chairs	pillows or beanbag chairs	glue, or glue sticks
pencils, crayons	paper	scissors
text sets	trade books	computer(s) and software
filmstrip projector	dictionaries and/or picture dictionaries	
encyclopedias	audiotapes prepared by an educator or child	

a variety of story cassette tapes and books

Big Books and multiple copies of smaller editions

cassette player/recorder, blank tapes

Math Center

This is a place for children of all levels to work together practicing skills in counting, comparing, measuring, sorting, and computing to solve counting problems.

Basic Supplies

games	beads	stopwatch
measuring tapes	rulers	number charts
paper and pencils	graph paper	computer

assorted manipulatives (pattern blocks, counting objects, one-inch cubes, Multilink cubes, Unifix cubes)

Art Center

Creativity, following directions, fine motor skills, and problem solving are further developed in this center. The art activities can be related to the theme, to holidays, or to shared literary experiences. They provide a means for the less verbal child to communicate ideas.

Basic Supplies

table	newspaper	plastic cover
paper	smocks	drying area
clay	crayons	paints, paintbrushes
tape	dictionary	source of water
markers	glue or glue sticks	scissors
stapler	hole punch	

Discovery Center

This center emphasizes math, science, and social studies. Children can explore and make observations independently that extend concepts presented during large-group instruction.

Basic Supplies

Materials and supplies will change depending on the subtheme. They may include:

magnifying lenses	rulers	tweezers
buckets, pans	magnets	paper and pencils
soil, pots, shovels	globes	dictionary
games	laminated maps	

Sand and Water Center

This center provides experiences that allow the children to explore concepts in measuring, comparing, problem solving, and story mapping. Instructions are given by the educator that lead the children into exploring, discovering, and drawing their own conclusions.

Basic Supplies

sand and water table   molds (letters, shapes)   containers of various sizes

digging tools   paper and pencils

small figurines, cars, houses, and other manipulatives

Cooking Experiences

Each subtheme unit includes an idea for a culminating cooking experience. The necessary materials and ingredients are listed. If an oven is not accessible for some of the cooking experiences, consider adapting the menu while keeping with the overall theme.

Assessing Student Performance

The focus of assessment in *Literature-Based Thematic Activities* is on the process of learning rather than on the product. More teachers are using performance assessments to measure what really counts—to what degree children apply their knowledge, skills, and understanding in real-life contexts (McTighe, 1996/1997). To assess the process by which students go about their play and solving problems in the classroom, educators must become good observers of child behavior.

In an active learning environment, there are numerous opportunities for observing and evaluating student performance as children are constantly engaged in speaking, listening, writing, reading, problem solving, and exploring. These activities provide many opportunities to evaluate students' attitudes about learning and how they see themselves as learners.

Sharing and planning sessions are central to the success of this active-learning environment approach. These sharing sessions provide additional opportunities for assessing children's skills. In these large-group situations, children reveal their curiosity, their ability to express themselves, their background of experiences, their creativity, and their ability to think logically and critically—just to name a few of the observable behaviors. Within each subtheme unit, activities that especially lend themselves to evaluating student performance are followed by an *Assessment Tip*, which is framed. These tips recommend strategies for informally observing students' work and performance.

Asking questions and informal talks, one on one, with students in the learning centers provide yet another way for educators to gain more information about the child's thinking and learning. In an active learning environment, educators have more opportunities to improve their observational skills and to know their children better than in the traditional classroom.

A third alternative for assessing student progress is to save samples of children's work throughout the year and keep them in a portfolio. Periodically collect samples of children's art, writing, or storytelling samples. Tape-record the child reading and use the tape to demonstrate reading development. Date each sample, and place into a permanent folder (portfolio) which may be used to observe student progress. Keep the portfolio.

Encourage students, periodically, to select their best examples of work to be placed in their portfolios. These performance records provide educators and parents with concrete, valuable information about each child's academic growth. Remember to celebrate a child's progress. McTighe (1996/1997) suggests sponsoring a portfolio party where families are invited to review students' work in the portfolios.

For students to take more responsibility for their own learning, they should become involved in self-assessment at an early age. In one-on-one discussions with children, discuss areas of improvement and help them develop new goals for the future. Children should be encouraged to reflect on their performance. Centers provide an ideal setting for children to begin the practice of self-assessment. *My Week in Centers*, found in Appendix A, was designed to help young children keep track of their center activities. Students are asked to think about the activity they enjoyed most and to write about it or draw a picture showing the activity. *My Week in Centers* can be saved in students' portfolios. Over time, the forms can reveal a pattern of interests. A copy of the form can go home with the child at the end of each school week. Having the form in hand will enable children to share with parents their activities in centers. It can also be of value as new centers are planned for students.

For more information about authentic assessment of this nature, the following resources are recommended:

Harp, B. (1991). *Assessment in Whole Language Programs and Evaluation.* Norwood, MA: Christopher Gordon.

Herman, J., Aschbacher, P., and Winters, L. (1992). *A Practical Guide to Alternative Assessment.* Alexandria, VA: Association for Supervision and Curriculum Development.

Scherer, M. (Ed.). (1996/1997). Teaching for Authentic Student Performance [Entire issue]. *Educational Leadership, 54*(4).

Tierney, R., Carter, M., and Desai, R. (1991). *Portfolio Assessment in the Reading-Writing Classroom.* Norwood, MA: Christopher Gordon.

Finally, Meisels (1996/1997) suggests an alternative for authentic assessment: using developmental guidelines in the form of checklists. Checklists help to systematically assess a student's progress in distinct areas. The following assessment checklists are included in this resource. These checklists are found in Appendix A and may be reproduced for instructional use:

1. Learning Behaviors Checklist

2. Listening Checklist

3. Speaking Checklist

4. Reading Checklist

5. Writing Checklist

The checklists include a three-level mastery system (suggested by Meisels, 1996/1997)—*Not Yet, In Process,* and *Proficient.* This structure is appropriate for all students including those with special needs.

Sunrise to Sunset:
What Do I Do Every Day?

Overview

As the subtheme unit *Sunrise to Sunset* begins, the children are asked to think about these questions:

How long is a day?

How do I and other people keep track of time?

What tools do we use to keep track of time?

Why do we need to keep track of time?

"What do I do every day?" is the question that initiates the children's exploration of time. After reading *Jesse Bear, What Will You Wear?* (1986) by Nancy White Carlstrom, the children are encouraged to think about their daily activities. They soon realize that many of their routines follow a predictable pattern governed by the natural phenomena of day and night.

Most of the literature selections and related activities are designed to make the children aware of the clock as a tool for telling time and organizing the day. Two poems, "Please, Mr. Clock" (1988) by Jill Eggleton and "Hickory Dickory Dock," the Mother Goose nursery rhyme, provide the backdrop for helping children learn how to tell time. To help children feel how long a minute lasts, one-minute tasks are presented. The poem, "9:00 O'Clock For You!" (1992) by Toni Tortoriello, and the Big Book, *Ten, Nine, Eight* (1989) by Molly Bang, deal with bedtime routines.

"The Big Clock" nursery rhyme and the song, "The Syncopated Clock" (1950) by Leroy Anderson (lyrics by Mitchell Parish), offer a natural setting for introducing rhythm instruments, employing the concept of duration and musical beats. Children are invited to create and play their own musical patterns.

Sunrise to Sunset provides children with the necessary background information to move on to the next subtheme unit, *Marvelous Monday*. *Marvelous Monday* involves children in the study of the concept of a week.

Skills and Concepts

Listening/Speaking/Reading/Writing

Understand and use time concepts:

    night, day, morning, noon, week,

    hour, minute, second, midnight,

    a.m., p.m., clockwise, counter-

    clockwise

Rhyme words

Recognize purpose of question mark

Describe thoughts and observations in complete sentences

Listen attentively to readings

Create an innovation of a poem

Dictate and read sentences

Recite nursery rhymes or poems

Sequence events in a story

Write and record time

Log events in a journal

Math

Conduct a survey and record results

Chart information on a graph

Count backwards from 10

Read time on the hour using a clock

Use a stopwatch to time activities

Estimate the time it takes to complete

    activities

Measure by using cups

Use musical instruments to count beats,

    to keep time, and to establish

    a rhythm

Recognize instruments used to measure

    time

Science

Determine the time it takes objects

    to sink and determine float time

Sort/categorize activities by day and

    night and by morning, noon, and

    night

Social Studies

Explore the concept of time zones

Work cooperatively in a small group

Understand how measures of time

    organize people's lives

Planning Ahead

Supplies to Gather

Experience chart and paper

Large demonstration clock

Small demonstration clocks,
   one per child

Index cards

8½" x 11" sheets of paper

Sentence strips (or tagboard cut into
   3" x 17" strips)

Rhythm instruments such as drums,
   sticks, tambourines, triangles, bells

Large and small paper fasteners

Tagboard to create a Big Book

Flashlight

Globe

Stopwatches or clocks/watches with
   second hands

Numbered necklaces, one per child
   (necklaces numbered 1–12)

Glue or glue sticks

Bean bag(s)

Props for the story *Corduroy*

Scissors

Cassettes/cassette player

Sheet music for "The Syncopated Clock" or musical CD (such as "Syncopated
   Clock and Other Favorites" by LeRoy Anderson, available from Intersound,
   1-612-349-2713)

Hammer

Nail

Cutting board

Bottle caps, at least four per child

Small tub filled with water

Broken clocks, watches

Paper plates

Construction paper to form hands of
   clock

Paper cup

Ruler

Marking pen

Glass jar or clear plastic bottle (wide
   mouth)

Rubber bands

Pitcher of water

Two detergent bottles (optional)

Screw (optional)

Cooking supplies (rice cakes, peanut
   butter, cream cheese, raisins,
   licorice laces, and plastic knives)

Mural paper

Books

Jesse Bear, What Will You Wear? (1986) by N.W. Carlstrom, New York: Macmillan.

What Makes Day and Night (1986) by F.M. Branley, New York: Crowell.

Books containing poetry about time (see pages 46–47)

Ten, Nine, Eight (1989) by M. Bang, Toronto: Scholastic.

Corduroy (1968) by D. Freeman, New York: Viking.

Books of nursery rhymes

Alternate read-aloud selections (see page 50)

Little Red Riding Hood (1983) by T.S. Hyman, New York: Holiday House.

The Little Red Hen (1973) by P. Galdone, New York: Houghton Mifflin/Clarion.

Games

Two bean bags of different colors

Pages to Duplicate

Please, Mr. Clock, pages 59–60, one per child

My Hickory, Dickory, Dock Rhyme, page 61, one per child and extras for the reading center

A New Syncopated Clock, page 62, one per child

Whole Notes/Half Notes, page 63, one per child and extras for the discovery center

How Long Did It Take?, page 64, copies for the reading center

How Long Does It Take?, page 65, copies for the math center

Sinking Caps, page 66, copies for the math center

Cap Experiments, page 67, copies for the math center

Sharing: From Invitations to Celebrations

1. A Typical Day

Ask the children to close their eyes and imagine one day. To help them visualize, talk them through a typical day. Here is one example, but individualize the routine to match your children's experiences as much as possible:

The alarm rings. It's time to get up.

You get dressed and have breakfast.

You climb aboard the school bus or walk to school.

At school, you spend the day in activities like reading, solving math problems, playing outside, and having lunch.

After school, you play with your friends outside until dinner time.

You do your homework quickly without needing any help.

Taking a bath or shower makes you feel so sleepy.

You get into bed. Dad or Mom reads your favorite bedtime story.

2. Daytime/Nighttime Activities

Divide a large sheet of chart paper into two columns. Label one column *Daytime*, and the other column *Nighttime*. Ask children to think of the various activities that occur throughout the day. As they name the activities, record them on the chart paper. As the children volunteer suggestions, ask them to tell you where to write the activity ("Shall I write it under *Nighttime* or under *Daytime?*"). Some activities may be placed under both headings.

Give each child a sheet of paper to be divided in half. Ask the children to illustrate daily events on one side and nighttime events on the other side. Encourage children to talk about day/night activities with their peers as they work. Provide time for the children to share their drawings with partners or in small groups. Save the children's work; it will be used for *Grouping by Day/Night* (see page 36).

3. What We Know About Night and Day

Help children discuss what they know about night and day by asking them questions such as, "How do we know when it is day or night?" Through discussion, they will reveal what perceptions, concepts, and knowledge they have about this natural phenomenon. Record their observations on large chart paper under the heading *What We Know or Think We Know*. Some examples are: "Night is dark, we see the stars at night, that's when we sleep."

Ask children, "What do we want to learn about day or night?" Record their responses on another sheet of chart paper under the heading *What We Want to Learn*. Some example responses might be: "How long is daytime? Where does the moon go? Do animals sleep at night? How do we know when it is time to get up?" By returning to the same questions for several days in a row and recording the children's observations, you will increase their interest and stimulate questions about the topic.

Prepare a third chart titled, *What We Have Learned About Time*. Hang all three charts in a prominent place. Return to them throughout the unit to confirm or refute the children's initial observations as they read and learn more about day and night and the clock as a tool for tracking 24 hours.

As soon as you initiate the topic, begin reading books about day and night. See the *Alternate Read-Aloud Selections* (page 50) for lists of books.

Shared Reading/Writing Experiences

Jesse Bear, What Will You Wear?

1. Read Aloud

Jesse Bear, What Will You Wear? (1986) by Nancy White Carlstrom uses rhyming verse to describe a typical day for Jesse Bear. Have children tell about the things they like to do on a warm sunny day.

Introduce *Jesse Bear, What Will You Wear?* by reading the title and the author's name. Ask the children what they think the story is about. Record their predictions on large chart paper. Read the predictions on the chart paper and point to the text to encourage the children to read along.

Note that the title is asking a question. Point out the punctuation. Ask the children to listen to find out who is asking the question.

Read the book without stopping. Return to the children's original predictions. Read them aloud, and ask the children to read along from the chart. Check the predictions that are true, and cross out those that do not apply. Reread the book, and encourage children to make comments about the book as you read it.

Discuss who asked the question, "What will you wear?" and who gave the answers. Through discussion, help the children realize that the question, "What will Jesse wear?" is a playful way to show what Jesse did throughout the day.

2. What Jesse Bear Did

On the chalkboard, write "What Jesse Bear Did." Then write the words, *In the morning, At noon, At night.*

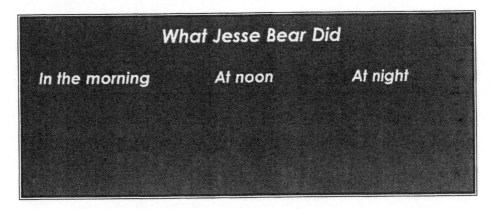

When creating lists or writing words, use the opportunity to demonstrate sound segmentation. For instance, when writing the word morning, ask

children to help you spell the word. One useful technique is to make a box for each letter and fill in the letter names in the correct box.

m			n			g

Ask the children, "What time is it when it's morning? When it is noon? When it is night?" If necessary, reread *Jesse Bear, What Will You Wear?* Ask the children to name Jesse's activities. Record these in appropriate categories.

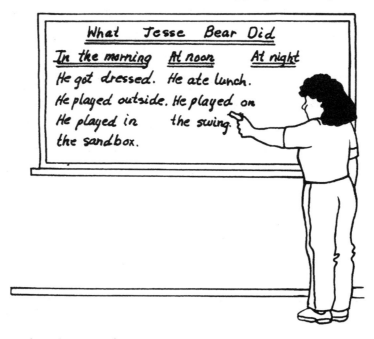

3. Grouping by Day/Night

Have children return to their drawings of day/night activities (see page 33). Invite them to categorize their activities by time into three groups: morning, noon, night. Instead of redrawing the illustrations, have them either write words naming the activities illustrated or cut, paste, and categorize the original drawings on another sheet of paper.

4. Jesse Bear Rhyme

The text of *Jesse Bear, What Will You Wear?* is in rhyme. When children are very familiar with the text and are able to read along, have them identify the rhyming words. Make a separate list of rhyming word pairs.

Return to this list on other occasions. Read it with the children, and add other rhyming words that are not in the text. Encourage the children to add rhyming words independently. When they do, take time to have children share these additions with their peers.

Rhyming Words
red-head
pants-dance-ants
run-sun
chair-there
peas-please
crunch-bunch
shirt-dirt
float-boat

5. **Puzzle Rhyming Game**

For homework, ask children to think of four sets of time rhyming words. (Invite families to help children hear and think of the rhyming words.)

Give children some samples of rhyming pairs, such as:

day—pay   night—fright   noon—spoon   time—dime

When most children have brought in their rhyming pairs, ask each child to choose two sets of rhyming words. Encourage the children to choose words that no one else in the class thought of. Give each child a long strip of paper or a sentence strip. Ask each child to write one rhyming word on the left side of the

day	pay
night	fright
noon	spoon
time	dime

paper and the other rhyming word on the right side of the paper.

Then have each child cut the sentence strip in two, using a unique cutting design. Have children form small groups and mix up their word strips. Have the children take turns matching the rhyming word pairs. Encourage them to help each other read the word pairs. Later, these puzzle pieces can be used at the reading center.

Favorite Rhymes about Time

1. Read Aloud

Write the following poems, "The Big Clock," "A Dillar, A Dollar, A Ten O'Clock Scholar" by Mother Goose and "Hickory, Dickory, Dock" on large sheets of chart paper. Read each poem several times. The children will enjoy the rhythm and rhyme of each poem.

The Big Clock

Slowly ticks the big clock;
Tick-tock, tick-tock!
But cuckoo clock ticks double quick;
Tick-a-tock-a, tick-a-tock-a,
Tick-a-tock-a, tick!

—*Author unknown*

**A Dillar, A Dollar,
A Ten O'Clock Scholar**

A dillar, a dollar, a ten o'clock scholar!
What makes you come so soon?
You used to come at ten o'clock,
But now you come at noon!

—*Mother Goose*

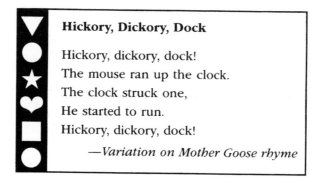

Hickory, Dickory, Dock

Hickory, dickory, dock!
The mouse ran up the clock.
The clock struck one,
He started to run.
Hickory, dickory, dock!

—*Variation on Mother Goose rhyme*

When children know the text of each poem well and have had multiple opportunities to discuss what each poem means, suggest that each child choose one poem to memorize.

2. The Clock Strikes Two

Use a large demonstration clock to show the times mentioned in two of the poems, "Hickory, Dickory, Dock" and "Ten O'Clock Scholar." Substitute times in each poem. For "Hickory, Dickory, Dock," pretend that the clock struck 2:00, instead of 1:00, and change the word in verse four to rhyme with two. Continue making similar substitutions. Use the big demonstration clock to show various times. Read the poem with the new times. Present several follow-up lessons for reading a clock. This would be an appropriate time to introduce the unit about telling time presented in most primary math textbooks.

3. Tick, Tock, Mr. Clock

Write the following poem, "Please, Mr. Clock" (1988) by Eggleton on chart paper. This an excellent poem for chanting and demonstrating time.

Please, Mr. Clock

Please, Mr. Clock,

With your tick and your tock,

Tell me the time.

Breakfast time.

Please, Mr. Clock,

With your tick and your tock,

Tell me the time.

School time.

Please, Mr. Clock,

With your tick and your tock,

Tell me the time.

Lunch time.

Please, Mr. Clock,

With your tick and your tock,

Tell me the time.

Play time.

(Continued on next page)

"Please, Mr. Clock"–continued

Please, Mr. Clock,

With your tick and your tock,

Tell me the time.

Dinner time.

Please, Mr. Clock,

With your tick and your tock,

Tell me the time.

Bed time.

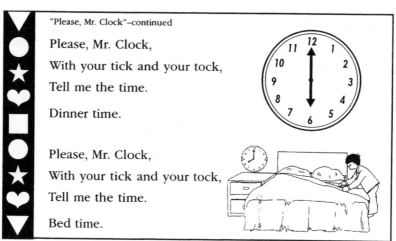

From *Now We Are Six*, by J. Eggleton, 1988, Bothell, WA: The Wright Group.
© 1988 by The Wright Group. Reprinted with permission.

Distribute one copy of "Please, Mr. Clock" (see pages 59–60) to each child. On the first page, instruct children to draw the hands on the clock to show the time they do the activities named in the poem. Read the poem as children complete this page. Then have the children use the second page to personalize the poem, changing the activities to ballet time, soccer time, bathtime, and so on. They can illustrate each page to show themselves involved in their special activities.

4. Tick Tock Rhythm

Supply rhythm instruments such as drums, sticks, and tambourines. Have the children chant "Please, Mr. Clock." Direct them to play their instruments when "tick" and "tock" are said. Write the poem again on large chart paper. Under the words, draw pictures of the instruments to be played. For example:

Please, Mr. Clock,

With your tick and your tock,

Tell me the time.

5. My Hickory, Dickory, Dock Rhyme

Distribute one copy of *My Hickory, Dickory, Dock Rhyme* (see page 61) to each child. Children love writing and reading their own poems by innovating on the original Mother Goose verse. Help the children fill in the blanks to create their

own poems. For example, children may change "Hickory, Dickory, Dock" in these ways:

Changing the name of the animal and the action:

Hickory, dickory, dock.
The elephant lumbered
up the clock

or

The snake wiggled
up the clock.

or

The kangaroo hopped up the clock.

Changing the time:

The clock struck ten,
He saw a big, old hen.

Children can also use a blank sheet of paper to rewrite the rhyme by changing initial consonants:

Stickory, slickory, spock!
The mouse ran up the clock.
The clock struck one.
He started to run.
Stickory, slickory, spock!

Other variations:

Rickory, wickory, tock!
-ickory, -ickory, -ock!

When completed, direct the children in stapling their silly poems together to make a class book. Name the book, number each entry, and make a Table of Contents page, listing children's names and page numbers of their poems.

Encourage children to write their innovations of "Hickory, Dickory, Dock" on large chart paper to hang in the reading center for all the children to read independently.

6. Big Book of "Hickory, Dickory, Dock"

Make a Big Book of "Hickory, Dickory, Dock" innovations. Use tagboard for the book cover. Draw a clock face on it. Use a large paper fastener attached to the middle for the hands on the clock. Children can take turns moving the hands showing the time mentioned in each poem.

7. Why Time?

Ask, "What do clocks and watches help us do?" Provide opportunities for the children to offer a variety of answers. Draw them to this conclusion: Clocks and watches help us tell time. Then ask, "Why do we need to know the time?" Again, provide time for the children to discuss this important concept.

When children begin to discover that using the clock helps to organize and plan the day, have them talk about situations that require knowing the hour, the day, and the month. List the situations on chart paper. Add situations over the next few days. Adding a few items each day allows the children to develop an awareness of how time affects their personal lives.

Copy and duplicate the completed list for each child. Show how to record time (6:00 o'clock, 7:00 o'clock). At school and for homework, have the children use the list to write the times that these events take place throughout the day. This assignment may require adult help. (Children do not have to record exact times to complete the assignment.)

Time to get up.

Time to meet the bus.

Time to watch a favorite TV program.

Time to go to lunch.

Time to go home.

Time to go to bed.

After the children have completed this assignment, use their work to show how *a.m.* and *p.m.* can be used instead of writing the phrases *in the morning, in the afternoon*, or *at night*.

8. Our Day at School

For one day, attempt to log all classroom events and the times they occur. Write them on chart paper. This activity will serve as a demonstration for writing time. Hang the completed chart in a prominent place so children can use it to create individual books or a class book titled *Our Day at School.* Encourage the children to illustrate their books and write statements about the events.

9. Day and Night

Discuss that a day is divided into day and night, each being 12 hours long. Twelve o'clock noon and twelve o'clock midnight are the dividing points. Read and show the pictures in *What Makes Day and Night* (1986) by Franklyn Branley, and read other books about day and night. Begin a fact sheet by recording important information as it is discussed and learned. Ask the children for help in selecting facts to be recorded. Children may want to begin their own fact sheets or journals about day and nights.

10. What We Know/Learned

Periodically reread the *What We Know, What We Want...* charts (see page 34) to help children keep track of their questions and to note whether their questions have been answered.

11. How Day and Night Occur

Use a flashlight and a globe to illustrate how day and night occur. Follow up the demonstration by asking children to select partners.

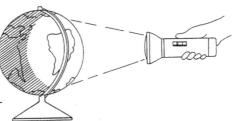

In pairs, have children take turns role-playing the sun and Earth. Tell the "sun" to remain still while Earth rotates on its axis (the Earth child slowly turns in place). Give the child who represents the Earth an index card with the word *day* written on it, so that when Earth is facing the sun, the card can be read by the sun child. On Earth's back, tape a card with the word *night* written on it. Have all the children in the classroom read this card.

Assessment Tip

The children's level of understanding will be revealed when they have to offer explanations using their own vocabulary and illustrations. This form of evaluation is very effective. Use it routinely.

12. A Day at School Pantomime

Refer to the class list of activities charted during *Our Day at School* (see page 43). Tell each child to select one activity and time from the chart and to copy it onto an index card. Use these cards to play a pantomime game.

Seat the children in a circle. Display a large demonstration clock, and provide a small demonstration clock for each child. Place the index cards in a pile in the center of the circle. Invite one child to take a card from the pile and act out the activity while the other children guess what the child is doing and at what time. Have the children show the time on their own small clocks. When the children are finished guessing, tell the first child to read the card and use the large demonstration clock to show the time written on the card. The other children should check their small clocks for accuracy.

13. "Big Clock" Rhythm

Reread the poem "The Big Clock" (see page 38). Divide the class into two groups. Ask one group to read lines 1 and 2 very slowly, and the other group to read lines 3, 4, and 5 quickly.

After children have had a chance to practice this activity several times, suggest repeating the activity using musical instruments. Write "The Big Clock" poem again on chart paper; this time showing children which rhythm instrument to play and how often. For example:

Slowly ticks the big clock,

Tick   –   tock,   tick   –   tock!

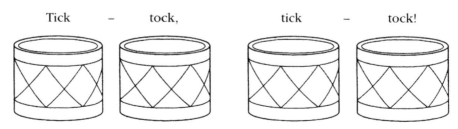

But cuckoo clock ticks double quick;

Tick-a-   tock-a,   tick-a   tock-a

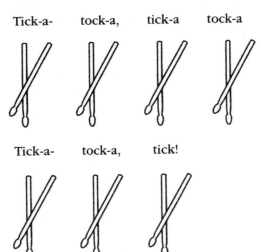

Tick-a-   tock-a,   tick!

"Time to Rise"

1. Read Aloud

Write the following poem, "Time To Rise" (1885) by Robert Louis Stevenson, on large chart paper.

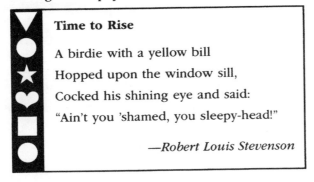

Time to Rise

A birdie with a yellow bill
Hopped upon the window sill,
Cocked his shining eye and said:
"Ain't you 'shamed, you sleepy-head!"

—*Robert Louis Stevenson*

Read and reread the poem. Then create a chart, such as the following, on mural paper, and display it on a bulletin board. Ask children to find out what time they get up every morning for school. Have them record the time on the chart. They can also write their moods when they wake up, and how they wake up. For a variation, instead of writing their names in the appropriate columns have the children attach small photos of themselves.

What time do you get up?

5:00	5:30	6:00	6:30	7:00	7:30	8:00
Jerry	Patti	Kari	Bob	Vera		
			Daisy			

In the morning, are you a sleepy head?

Yes	No
Patti	Jerry
Bob	Vera
	Daisy
	Kari

How do you wake up?

Alarm clock	I
Clock radio	II
Parent	I
Sunlight	II

Assessment Tip

Organizing information on a chart presents a tremendous opportunity to watch children apply mathematical concepts such as estimating, adding, subtracting, and communicating data using the terms *more, less,* and *equal.* Make note of those children who seem advanced or who seem to have difficulty.

Read other poems about time. Some examples are:

"Wee Willie Winkie" from *Wee Willie Winkie and Other Rhymes* (1976) by Iona Opie, Cambridge, MA: Candlewick.

Poems from *Anthology of Children's Literature* (1976), by May Hill Arbuthnot, Glenview, IL: Scott Foresman.

"Moon-Come-Out" and "Waking Time" by Eleanor Farjeon from *Eleanor Farjeon's Poems for Children* (1984), Philadelphia, PA: Lippincott.

"Clock" by Valerie Worth from *The Poetry Troupe* (1977), compiled by Isabel Wilner, New York: Scribner.

"Never Too Late" by Aileen Fisher from *I Wonder How and Why* (1962), New York: Abelard-Schuman.

"Is It Robin O'Clock?" by Eve Merriam from *Blackberry Ink* (1985), New York: Morrow.

Ten, Nine, Eight

1. Read Aloud

Read the book *Ten, Nine, Eight* (1989) by Molly Bang. Children enjoy counting along as you read this beautifully illustrated book. A little girl preparing to go to bed lovingly counts things in her room, going backward from 10 to 1. Read the book aloud several times.

2. Rhyming Pairs

Ask the children to help you find the rhyming pairs in the text. List those words on chart paper. Hang the chart paper in the writing center and invite children to add more rhyming pairs.

3. Bedtime Countdown

For homework, children will enjoy creating their own bedtime countdown by finding and counting objects 10 to 1 in their bedrooms. Have them write a statement or draw a picture for each item on a separate piece of paper. Tell them to record the number of items on each page. On the last page of the book, have children write the time they go to bed or draw a clock showing the time. When the assignment is completed, staple the papers in numerical order to form a book. Be sure to save time for children to share their work.

4. Counting Backwards

Children love to count backward. It is an excellent presubtraction activity. Practice it daily. Have the children clap, slap their thighs, or hop as they count.

"9:00 O'Clock For You!"

1. Read Aloud

Write the following poem, "9:00 O'Clock for You!" (1992) by Toni Tortoriello, on chart paper. Read the poem to the children.

9:00 O'Clock for You!

Five minutes more
That's all I ask.
Is this too much
For the child you adore?

I must see the end of this TV show.
Then straight upstairs, I promise I'll go.
I'll wash my face, brush my teeth,
Jump into bed, and turn out the light.

Promise!

It's not fair, you know.
My friend Nicole can stay up till 9:30.
Kristy can too.
But me oh, no.
You say, "9:00 for you!"

One of these nights I'd like to try
And stay up so late until I cry…
"I'm going to BED!"
But I know this can't come true.
Because you always say, "9:00 for you!"

—*Toni Tortoriello*

---

2. Bedtime Excuses

Have the children discuss, write about, or list all the excuses they use for not going to bed. Have each child dramatize their bedtime excuses. How many more minutes does each child ask for?

3. How Long Is a Minute?

Plan several demonstrations to give children a sense of how long a minute lasts. For example, ask the children to do these tasks for one minute (be sure to point out the second hand moving on the clock as you time the minute):

- Extend your arm forward, and hold it there.
- Write your name.
- Say the ABCs.
- Hop on one foot.
- Snap your finger.
- Say a poem.
- Write as many numbers as possible.
- Write as many words as possible.

Challenge the children to think of other activities they could do for one minute.

Have children take turns being the timekeeper for the one-minute tasks while other children perform the tasks. Repeat these one-minute tasks several times during the week.

Corduroy

1. Read Aloud

Read the book *Corduroy* (1968) by Don Freeman. Discuss the events of the story. Have children name 10 story events. Do not require that the events be named in any sequence. Write the events on sentence strips. (For younger children, illustrate the events in some way.)

2. *Corduroy* Events Sequence

Divide the class into groups of three or four. Give each group a sentence strip. Allow children time to line up (organize) according to the sequence of events in the story. Help them organize using time concepts *before, after, next,* etc. Read the story again and have each small group hold their sentence strip up when you read the corresponding event from the story. Decide as a large group if the class had sequenced the events appropriately.

Alternate Read-Aloud Selections

All In a Day (1986) by Mitsumasa Anno and Raymond Bri, New York: Philomel.
This book describes what children in eight different countries are doing at the same time over a 24-hour period. The similarities and differences reveal the commonality of humankind.

The Way to Start a Day (1978) by Byrd Baylor, Old Tappan, NJ: Macmillan.
Turn to the east and welcome the day with beautiful poetry.

Keeping Time (1993) by Franklyn Branley, Boston, MA: Houghton Mifflin.
Special activities, folklore, and science are combined in this guide to everything about time (e.g., who named the weekdays, why an hour has 60 minutes).

The Shopping Basket (1980) by John Burningham, Cambridge, MA: Candlewick.
Children will discover what takes Stephen so long when he goes shopping.

The Best Time of Day (1979) by Valerie Flournoy, New York: Harper.
An Afro-American family shares good times.

Clocks and More Clocks (1970) by Pat Hutchins, New York: Macmillan.
None of the clocks in this story read the same time. Children will discover why.

Time to... (1989) by Bruce McMillan, New York: Lothrop, Lee, and Shepard.
This is a wonderful book of clock photographs depicting a typical day for a young child with an hour-by-hour introduction to telling time.

No Bath Tonight (1989) by Jane Yolen, New York: Harper.
This book is about the days of the week.

Say Good Night (1987) by Harriet Ziefert, New York: Viking Penguin.
Parents need to convince their little girl that night is good.

Songs, Movement, and Games

Song

1. "The Syncopated Clock"

Children will enjoy learning "The Syncopated Clock" (1950) by Leroy Anderson. (Borrow the sheet music from your music department or use a CD or audio-cassette of the music.) Besides the appealing story and wonderful lyrics (by

Mitchell Parish), the music provides an excellent opportunity to introduce musical notes and use rhythm instruments. Rhythm is a "timing" concept that easily works into a "time" theme.

Write the lyrics on large chart paper. Hang it in a prominent place. Read the lyrics and discuss the meaning of the song. Sing the song.

Refer to the lyrics and help children identify rhyming pairs. Note that some of the words that rhyme end with the same letter while other pairs do not. Record the rhyming words that end with the same letters on a separate chart.

Distribute one copy of *A New Syncopated Clock* (see page 62) to each child. Have them complete the activity and share their rhyming pairs.

Refer to the second stanza of "The Syncopated Clock" on the chart paper. Let the children clap their hands and snap their fingers to accompany this verse. For example:

Tick-	a-	tock,	tick-	a-	tock,
Clap	clap	clap	Clap	clap	clap

There's a zing in the swing of that clock

Tock-	a-	tick,	tock-	a-	tick,
Snap	snap	snap	Snap	snap	snap

Don't you think it's a marvelous trick?

Ting-	a-	ling,	ting-	a-	ling,
Snap	clap	snap	Snap	clap	snap

There's a zong in the bong of that ring.

Ling-	a-	ting,	ling-	a-	ting,
Clap	snap	clap	Clap	snap	clap

Don't you think it's a wonderful thing?

When children can successfully clap and snap, ask them to make suggestions for changing the clap/snap pattern. Introduce percussion instruments— drums, sticks, triangles, and bells—to be used instead of clapping and snapping. See the example on page 52.

2. Objects that Make Rhythm

Invite children to collect the names of objects that use a beat or regularly patterned sound (for example, phones, clock, microwave, windshield wipers). Write these items on chart paper and invite children to continue to add to the list during this subtheme unit.

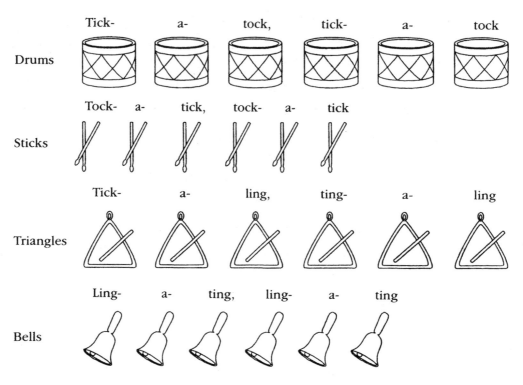

Drums — Tick- a- tock, tick- a- tock

Sticks — Tock- a- tick, tock- a- tick

Triangles — Tick- a- ling, ting- a- ling

Bells — Ling- a- ting, ling- a- ting

3. Whole Note/Half Note Beat

Introduce musical notes. Reproduce many copies of the *Whole Notes/Half Notes* activity page (see page 63) so children can cut and paste them to create their own musical patterns. Demonstrate how to do this by cutting out four notes and arranging them in a pattern. Then show children how they can clap/snap the pattern or choose one or two rhythm instruments to play the musical pattern. Explain that the whole note represents a sustained beat. The half note is held for half the amount of time; two beats (count to 2) equal a whole note. For example:

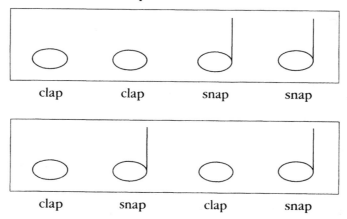

clap   clap   snap   snap

clap   snap   clap   snap

Leave copies of *Whole Notes/Half Notes* in the discovery center for children to use to create their own musical patterns.

Movement

1. Natural Rhythm

Have children illustrate natural rhythms through physical movement, such as galloping, running, jumping, and skipping. Challenge children to use paper musical notes to create a pattern imitating the physical activity.

Games

1. What Time Is It, Mr. Fox?

This outdoor game is similar to "Red Light, Green Light." The educator (or a child) is Mr. Fox. The children stand 25 to 30 feet away from Mr. Fox. The children call out, "What time is it, Mr. Fox?" The fox replies by giving a specific time (e.g., "It's 2 o'clock"). The children walk toward Mr. Fox, taking the number of steps equal to the time Mr. Fox mentioned (in this case, 2 steps).

Whenever Mr. Fox says, "It's 12 o'clock," he chases the children. Any child tagged stands with Mr. Fox and becomes a fox pup ready to chase and tag other children when Mr. Fox says, "It's 12 o'clock."

2. Bean Bag Clock

Twelve children form a circle, representing a clock. Each child is given a numbered necklace, starting with 12, then 1, 2, and so on. While music is playing, the children pass a bean bag clockwise around the circle. When the music stops, the child holding the bag announces the hour (i.e., the number of his or her necklace).

Variations:

A child who is standing in the center of the circle announces the hour based on which child is left holding the bean bag when the music stops.

Two beans bags of different colors are used. One bean bag represents the hour, the other bean bag the minutes. In this case, necklaces will also need to be numbered to represent minutes.

3. Hot Bean Bag

This game is a variation of "Hot Potato." Children stand in a circle anal pass the bean bag from one person to the next while music is playing. When the music stops, the person holding the bag is eliminated. Use a CD player, radio,

or audiotape for music. Turn the volume low to catch a child holding the bean bag. Vary the length of time the music is played. Alternate passing the bag *clockwise* and *counterclockwise* to help the children learn these terms.

4. Bean Bag Records

For this game, the children form a circle. They pass a bean bag around the circle without dropping it. Time how long it takes to pass the bean bag around one time. Tell them how long it took. Challenge children to pass the bean bag faster around the circle without dropping it. Repeat the activity until a record for the shortest time is achieved. Records usually are broken. The children may wish to issue a challenge to other classrooms; or they may want to form smaller circles and compete against one another.

Learning Centers

Drama Center

1. Drama of *Corduroy*

Have available props such as teddy bears, buttons, stuffed animals, and dolls so children can dramatize the story *Corduroy*.

2. Pantomime

Have children pantomime daily activities while other children guess the activity and the time of day it occurs.

3. Nursery Rhyme Drama

Display nursery rhyme books and tell children to recite the nursery rhymes to each other.

4. Drama of "9:00 O'Clock for You!"

Post the chart paper with the poem "9:00 O'Clock for You!" in the drama center. Encourage children to take turns dramatically reading the poem.

Writing Center

1. Daily Activities

Tell children to list the things they do daily. When the list is completed, have them keep their lists handy for one day to record the times each activity is done.

2. More Rhyming Words

Have available the chart paper of rhyming words begun in *Rhyming Pairs* (see page 47). Invite children to add to the list of rhyming words.

Reading Center

1. Read to Find Out

Display the books *Little Red Riding Hood, The Little Red Hen, Corduroy,* and a book of nursery rhymes. After children read the stories, they should decide the period of time each story or event encompasses. Show them how to record their answers on *How Long Did It Take?* (see page 64). Encourage the children to add their own event from a story to the first column.

2. "Hickory, Dickory, Dock" Poems

Have available large chart paper for children to write original poems based on "Hickory, Dickory, Dock." Help them hang their poems in the reading center for everyone to read. Laminated poetry hanging in the reading center is an invitation to all children to read.

3. Book Display

Display class books, Big Books, and trade books about time (see the Alternate Read-Aloud Selections on page 50 and pages 46–47 for example poetry about time).

4. *Corduroy*

Provide an audiotape of the book of *Corduroy*.

5. Rhyming Word Puzzles

Invite children to work together to complete the rhyming word puzzles created during the *Puzzle Rhyming Game* (see page 37).

Math Center

1. How Long Does It Take?

Tell children to work in pairs to determine how long it takes to perform simple tasks. Have available copies of *How Long Does It Take?* (see page 65). Help

children read the list of activities. Ask one child to estimate (guess) how long it takes to complete each activity and record the guess in the first column next to the activity. Instruct that child to then perform each activity while another child times the activity with a watch or stopwatch, and enters the correct amount of time in the second column. (It may take several days to complete all the activities and fill in the questions at the bottom of the activity page.)

2. One-Minute Tasks

Tell children to choose a partner. Have the pairs list five things they think they can do in one minute. While one child performs the activity, the other times the activity with a watch or stopwatch. Do not expect accuracy when children time events. These exercises will give them practice in using time in a practical situation, applying the vocabulary of time and recording time.

3. Clock Survey

Tell children to survey how many digital and how many regular (analog) clocks are in school and in their homes. Have children share their results with the large group.

4. Sinking Caps

(Note: This activity requires adult help.)

Provide four bottle caps per child and one copy of *Sinking Caps* (see page 66). Using a hammer, a nail, and a cutting board, show children how to punch holes into their four bottle caps. Instruct children to punch one hole in the first cap, two holes in the second cap, three in the third cap, and four in the fourth one. Children should label each cap with their names and the number of holes in the cap (e.g., *Steven 2*). Then have them take turns placing their caps in a small tub filled with water and observe which caps sink first, second, third, and fourth. Have stopwatches or clocks with second hands available so children can time how long it takes each cap to sink. They should record the results on their copy of *Sinking Caps*.

To discover which cap remains afloat the longest, tell children to then test their best caps against one another's best caps. They should use the activity page, *Cap Experiments* (see page 67) to record the results (remind them how to record the names of the caps). The process continues until one or two caps are identified as being the ones that float the longest.

5. Clock Collection

Encourage children to begin a clock collection. They can bring to school a variety of watches, timepieces, and clocks to examine, sort, and classify.

Discovery Center

1. Day/Night Discovery

Provide a globe and flashlight. Encourage children to repeat the experiment, *How Day and Night Occur,* demonstrated earlier (see page 43).

2. Broken Clocks

Provide broken clocks and watches that can be pulled apart and the inner workings examined.

3. Musical Creation

Have available multiple copies of *Whole Notes/Half Notes* (see page 63) so children can create their own musical patterns (as described on pages 52–53).

Art Center

1. Paper-Plate Clocks

Encourage children to make paper-plate clocks, using paper fasteners to attach hands created from construction paper.

Sand and Water Center

1. Water Clock

Children will be fascinated with the idea of developing a water clock.

For each clock you will need:

a paper cup

a nail

a hammer

a ruler

a marking pen

a glass jar or clear plastic bottle
(wide mouth)

rubber bands

a strip of paper

a pitcher of water

Punch a nail hole in the bottom of the paper cup. Mark off inches on the strip of paper. Attach the strip of paper to the jar with one or two rubber bands.

Place the paper cup in the opening of the jar. Pour water to the top of the cup. Time how long and how many cups it takes to fill the jar to one inch, two inches, three inches, and so on.

A similar experiment can be done with two detergent bottles. Keep the caps on. Cut each bottle lengthwise to create a bowl. Insert a screw just below the neck of one of the bottles. Fill one container with water. Place the second bottle under and below the bowl to catch the water. Remove the screw from the first bottle so that the water can flow out. Have children time how long it takes for the second container to fill.

Cooking Experiences

Rice Cake Clocks

rice cakes (one for each child)

peanut butter

cream cheese

raisins

licorice laces (one for each child)

plastic knives

paper plates

Give each child a paper plate and a rice cake. Ask the children to write their names on the paper plates. Provide a plastic knife to each child. Instruct children to spread cream cheese or peanut butter on their rice cakes. Then they should decorate their rice cakes with raisins and licorice to resemble a clock.

Before children eat their snacks:

1. Have the children take turns reading the time on their clocks and telling whether it is a significant time (e.g., bedtime).

2. Have the children create a graph by arranging their plates in two rows. One row is for clocks with faces of peanut butter, while the second row contains the clocks with faces made of cream cheese. Children compare rows to determine which row has more, fewer, or whether they are equal in number.

Eat and enjoy!

Name _____ **Date** _____

Please, Mr. Clock

Breakfast Time

School Time

Lunchtime

Play Time

Bedtime

Time to Wake Up

Name _____ **Date** _____

Please, Mr. Clock

_____

_____

_____

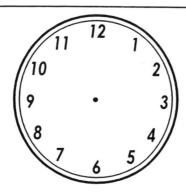

_____

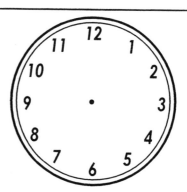

_____

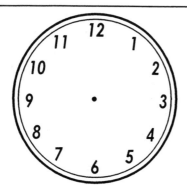

_____

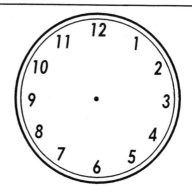

Name _____ **Date** _____

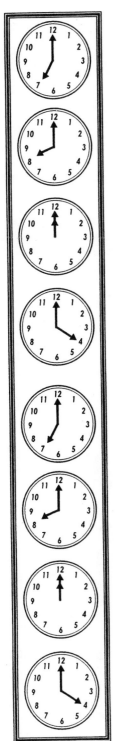

My Hickory, Dickory, Dock Rhyme

Hickory, dickory, dock!

The _____ _____ _____ the clock.

The clock struck _____.

He _____.

Hickory, dickory, dock!

Name _____ **Date** _____

A New Syncopated Clock

Fill in the missing letters. Then read the rhyming pairs.

me   b ___

king   t h ___ ___ ___

say   w ___ ___

flock   s ___ ___ ___

tick   t r ___ ___ ___

too   z ___ ___

race   p l ___ ___ ___

hock   s h ___ ___ ___

tock   c l ___ ___ ___

Name _____ **Date** _____

Whole Notes

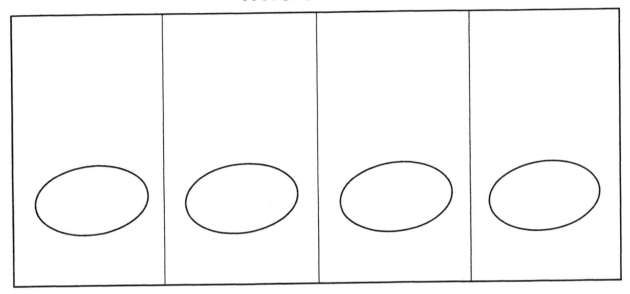

Half Notes

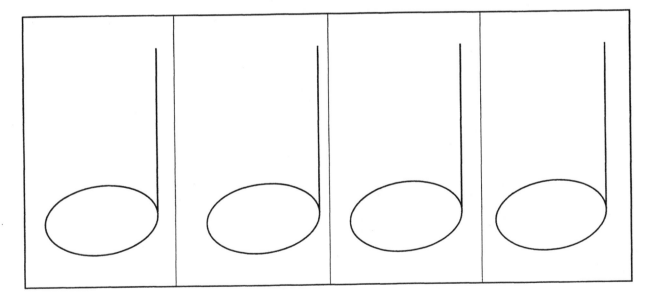

Name _____ **Date** _____

How Long Did It Take?

	A Year	A Month	A Week	A Day	An Hour	One Minute	One Second
The *Little Red Riding Hood* story to take place?							
The Little Red Hen to grow her seeds?							
For Humpty Dumpty to fall?							
For Corduroy to get a new button?							
The cow to jump over the moon?							
The Little Red Hen to bake her bread?							

Name _____ **Date** _____

How Long Does It Take?

	Guess How Long	How Long Did It Take?
Write the ABCs		
Walk to the door		
Skip to the door		
Play tic-tac-toe		
Play checkers		
Draw 6 △ s		
Draw 6 ◯ s		
Read a book		

Which activity took the longest time? _____

Which activity took the shortest time? _____

Think of 5 other things to do. Time how long they take to complete.

1. _____

2. _____

3. _____

4. _____

5. _____

Name _____ **Date** _____

Sinking Caps

Draw the number of holes in the caps.	How long did it take to sink?	
	Minutes	Seconds
First ⬡ **to sink.**		
Second ⬡ **to sink.**		
Third ⬡ **to sink.**		
Fourth ⬡ **to sink.**		

Which cap floated the longest?

Name _____ **Date** _____

Cap Experiments

Cap name Cap name	Record the best one here. How long did it float?
1. ⬭ **vs** ⬭	
2. ⬭ **vs** ⬭	
3. ⬭ **vs** ⬭	
4. ⬭ **vs** ⬭	
5. ⬭ **vs** ⬭	
6. ⬭ **vs** ⬭	
7. ⬭ **vs** ⬭	
8. ⬭ **vs** ⬭	

Marvelous Monday:
What Do I Do Weekly?

Overview

In the subtheme unit, *Marvelous Monday*, the children discuss their weekly activities. For one week, they keep track of school events. This activity paves the way for an exciting whole-group writing experience—the class newspaper. Children also are invited to start a daily journal.

The literature selected for *Marvelous Monday* involves the children in the unique experiences of people and animals going through their week. Children laugh as they read about the silly antics of Cookie, the cat, in *Cookie's Week* (1988) by Cindy Ward. In *The Very Hungry Caterpillar* (1983) by Eric Carle, children learn about what a hungry caterpillar eats each day of the week.

All activities in this subtheme unit will help children answer such questions as "How long is a week?"; "What are the names of the days of the week?"; and "How long do some activities take?"

Skills and Concepts

Listening/Speaking/Reading/Writing

Improve vocabulary development	Dictate and read sentences
Name the days of the week	Log activities in a journal
Order the days of the week	Understand cause and effect
Understand and use time concepts: yesterday, day before yesterday, tomorrow, day, week, today, month	Create illustrations or articles for a class newsletter
Categorize events as daily or weekly	Create an innovation of a poem
	Listen attentively to readings

Math

Collect data on a chart	Time events
Keep records for a week	Measure height in inches
Tally information in a short time span	

Science

Observe plant growth	Observe growth of mold
Identify sprouting	Measure evaporation
Observe sun movement as a measure of time	

Social Studies

Share events based on emotions	Work cooperatively in a small group
Use references to understand time/distance and geographical time zones	

Planning Ahead

Supplies to Gather

Experience chart and paper	Rubber bands
Blank books for daily journal	Plastic jar
Sentence strips (or tagboard cut into 3" x 17" strips)	Food coloring
	Compass
Seeds (e.g., bean, marigold, corn, tomato)	Clay
	Stick (about 6")
Large white plastic cloth	Cooking supplies (boxes of instant
Stopwatch	pudding, mixing spoon and bowl,
Water color paints	milk, bowls and spoons for eating
Variety of breads	pudding)
Graph paper	Colored markers
Toothpicks	(optional) Musical album *We All Live*
Maps or globes	*Together*, available from
Sheets of paper	Youngheart Records, 2413
Stuffed animals or puppets	Hyperion Ave., Los Angeles, CA
6" rulers	90027-4713 (213) 663-3223

Books

Guinness Book of World Records (1996) by Guinness Media, Stamford, CT: Author.

On Monday When It Rained (1989) by Cherryl Kachenmeister, Boston: Houghton Mifflin.

Cookie's Week (1988) by Cindy Ward, New York: Putnam.

The Very Hungry Caterpillar (1983) by E. Carle, New York: Philomel.

Various alternate read-aloud selections (see pages 79–80)

Reference books regarding time zones (e.g., phone book)

This Book Is About Time (1978) by Marilyn Burns, Boston, MA: Little, Brown.

Games

Hula-Hoops

Pages to Duplicate

On ___, When It ___, pages 86–87, several per small group

My Week, pages 88–89, one per child and extras for the writing center

What Did I Eat Today?, page 90, one per child and extras for the writing center

Yesterday and the Day Before, page 91, one per child

Time Tally, page 92, copies for the math center

Tracking Plant Growth, page 93, copies for the discovery center

Sharing: From Invitations to Celebrations

Begin this subtheme unit on either Monday or Friday.

1. The Days of the Week

As an introduction to the unit, hang seven large sheets of paper on a bulletin board or chalkboard. Ask the children, "Do you know the names of the days of the week?" As they name the days, write them on the chalkboard. When all the days of the week have been named, ask the children to help you write the name of a day on each large sheet. Have them help you decide in what order to arrange the charts. Then have children describe activities that may occur on each day.

Below the name of each day, record the anticipated activities for the day. At the end of the first day, reread the list for that day. With the children's involvement, check off the events that did in fact occur, cross out those that didn't happen, and add others that occurred. Repeat this activity each day. Children enjoy comparing activities from week to week.

This activity has two purposes. For younger students, maintaining a class log helps children realize the time span incorporated in one week. For older students, at the end of the week, the information collected can be used to create a newspaper called *Our Week in Review* (see pages 73–74). Children illustrate the newspaper, reproduce it, and take it home to parents.

2. Daily/Weekly Journals

Encourage children to create their own logs or journals of the day's or week's events. Children enjoy recording and/or illustrating daily events in small blank books and sharing them with classmates and parents. Many children probably will imitate the class model, so be sure to create one.

Invite children to think about and share the activities they do daily and weekly. Over a few days, write the children's activities on large chart paper. Hang the chart in a prominent place. Categorize events as daily and weekly.

Every Day (daily)

watch TV

take a bath

brush teeth

read with Mom or Dad

make my bed

Once a Week (weekly)

shop for food

go to Sunday School

clean my room

go to gym class

Shared Reading/Writing Experiences

1. Our Week in Review

Have the children plan and create a classroom newspaper, Using their ideas from daily charts started on page 72. Help the children realize all the possibilities, and guide the process by examining the *Weekly Reader*, local newspapers,

and various other models. By looking at models, children will begin to see how newspapers are organized. Begin conservatively by selecting only one or two news items. If children like the project, it can continue to grow and improve.

Decide how often the paper will be published, and brainstorm possible news items for the paper and write on chart paper. The newspaper can include examples of the children's drawings, poems, and stories. For younger children, it should include pictures of the children interacting or working at important activities. Be sure to emphasize important time concepts and when events occurred.

Possible News Items
school events
classroom events
playground
lunchroom news
child advice column

An editorial column offers children an opportunity to voice their opinions about happenings in the classroom and school. Older students can write one or two sentences. Younger students can dictate their ideas for an adult to write.

Invite parents, teachers, the principal, and other children to write "Letters to the Editor" or to contribute guest features. Have older children conduct interviews of school personnel. Demonstrate how to create good questions that children can use for interviewing people, and model how to use those questions to write a short article.

Once the process and format of the newspaper is established, move the project to the writing center. Have the children work on the newspaper there. Encourage the children to share ideas and articles with their classmates when center time is over. Be prepared for the children's interest in the class newspaper to wane. When children begin to lose interest, bring the project to a graceful end by planning a final issue.

On Monday, When It Rained

1. Read Aloud

In the book, *On Monday, When It Rained* (1989), Cherryl Kachenmeister, author, uses photographs of a preschooler to show the many emotions he experiences during one week. Remind students of the number of days in a week.

Invite children to look at the photograph on the cover, read the title, and tell what they think the book is about. Record their impressions and predictions on chart paper. Read the book. After reading two to three scenarios, the children will want to guess the emotion that matches the accompanying text.

Reread the book. Ask the children to recall the emotions the little boy felt. Record these on the chalkboard. Have children share times when they felt lonely, disappointed, or excited. Reinforce the concept of time span: hours, days, and weeks.

2. On ____, When ____ It

Distribute *On____, When____ It* book pages (see pages 86–87) to the children. Have the children create *On ____, When____ It* books in small groups. Have them think about situations and emotions they remember experiencing and draw self-portraits on the pages of the booklets. Then they should write how they felt, modeling the sentence pattern from *On Monday, When It Rained*. When all the members of the group are finished, have the group discuss how to arrange the pages of portraits and personal stories to create a book. Have one or two children create the cover for the book. Let the individual children read their own pages when they share the book with the class.

Cookie's Week

1. Read Aloud

Cookie's Week (1988) by Cindy Ward is a humorous account of a kitten's antics through the week, beginning with, "On Monday, Cookie fell in the toilet." This highly predictable book allows children to see the relationship between cause and effect.

Before reading the book, write several events from the book onto sentence strips. For each event, write the result of the action on another sentence strip. Tell children that the sentence strips are about events taken from the book. Read all the events first, and then read all the effects. Ask children to predict which event matches an effect. The following are examples:

Situation	Effect
On Monday, Cookie fell in the toilet.	There was water everywhere.
On Wednesday, Cookie upset the trash can.	There was garbage everywhere.
On Thursday, Cookie got stuck in a kitchen drawer.	There were pots and pans and dishes everywhere.

After the children have completed matching events with effects, ask them to put the events in order according to the days named. Ask children to name the missing days. Then have the children guess what other situations the kitten might experience. Read *Cookie's Week*.

2. My Week

After the children have heard *Cookie's Week* read several times, they might enjoy writing their own books, innovating on the text from *Cookie's Week*. Distribute *My Week* booklet pages (see pages 88–89) to the children. Help children write their stories and then give them time to illustrate. Keep extra copies of *My Week* in the writing center.

3. Journal Reading

Encourage children to reread the lists of daily and weekly events in their journals and class logs to create innovations based on personal events rather than pets.

The Very Hungry Caterpillar

1. Read Aloud

From the book *The Very Hungry Caterpillar* (1983) by Eric Carle, children are introduced to the days of weeks and what a very hungry caterpillar eats each day. Read the book two or three times.

2. What Did I Eat Today?

Suggest that the children keep track of what they—or their pets—eat daily and weekly. Have the children think of different methods for keeping track and help them develop a plan for collecting data.

One method is to record each day's food consumption on *What Did I Eat Today?* (see page 90). Distribute one copy to each child. Reinforce the concept of week and day. Point out any school lunch menus and have children decide if they represent a day, a week, or a month. Children can record their pets or their own diets in pictures as well as in written form.

"My Week"

1. Read Aloud

Before class, write the following poem, "My Week" (1998) by Sarah Tobalsky, on a large sheet of chart paper. Read the poem aloud. Ask, "What is the person doing today? What did the person do yesterday? The day before? What do you think the person will do tomorrow?"

My Week

Yesterday I played some baseball;
This is what I did:
I hit the ball and ran to first,
And, on my knees, I slid.

The day before, I went to soccer;
This is what I said:
"Kick the ball way up high;
I'll hit it with my head."

Today I have to go to dance class;
This is what I'll learn:
Point your toes, and stand up straight,
And do a ballet turn.

Tomorrow is a Saturday;
This is what I'll do:
Nothing, 'cause I'm tired from my week.
How about you?

—*Sarah Tobalsky*

2. **My Week Activities**

Invite children to dramatize the action described in each verse by pretending to play baseball, play soccer, and dance.

Ask children for a list of other activities the child in the poem might like trying (such as swimming, going to the zoo, and camping). Then write the poem on chart

Dance Class

Today I have to go to <u>dance</u> <u>class</u>;
This is what I'll <u>learn</u>:
<u>Point</u> <u>your</u> <u>toes</u>, <u>and</u> <u>stand</u> <u>up</u> <u>straight</u>,
<u>And</u> <u>do</u> <u>a</u> <u>ballet</u> <u>turn</u>.

The Zoo

Today I have to go to the zoo;
This is what I'll see:
A great, big bear; a tall giraffe;
And a cute monkey.

paper. Use the class suggestions to replace the underlined words in the poem with new activities. Read the poem with the new words.

3. Yesterday and the Day Before

Distribute one copy of *Yesterday and the Day Before* (see page 91) to each child. Point out that the days of the week are written around the edges of the page. Help children fill in the blanks regarding the time concepts. Point out that they can copy the day of the week from the edge of the paper. Using the pattern of the "My Week" poem, invite children to write (or draw the action word) for their own version.

Alternate Read-Aloud Selections

The Very Hungry Caterpillar (1987) by Eric Carle, New York: Philomel.

> A very hungry caterpillar eats a new item each day of the week; an introduction to the days of the week.

Some of the Days of Everette Anderson (1978) by Lucille Clifton, Cambridge, MA: Holt.

> This is a book of beautifully written poetry about a little boy's days.

Our Teacher, Miss Poole (1983) by Joy Cowley, New York: Owens.

> The teacher arrives to school in a different vehicle each day of the week.

Nathaniel Talking (1989) by Eloise Greenfield, New York: Writers and Readers.

> This is a charming book about a spirited nine-year-old poet who talks in rap about his day.

The Carrot Seed (1989) by Ruth Krauss. New York: Harper.

> A small boy plants his very own seed. He never doubts that it will sprout, even though everyone says it won't grow.

Jafta and the Wedding (1989) by Hugh Lewin and Lisa Kopper, Minneapolis, MN: Carolrhoda Books.

> In an African village, everyone has a job to do each day of the week to get ready for a wedding.

Fox All Week (1978) by Edward Marshall, New York: Dial Books.

> Weekly events are humorously described through Fox's adventures.

"Fox and the Girls" (1982) from *Fox in Love* by Edward Marshall, New York: Dial Books.

> Fox meets a different lovely fox each day of the week.

My Bike (1982) by Craig Martin, New York: Owens.

> Each day of the week brings a new episode for a young boy riding his bike.

When I Was Young in the Mountains (1982) by Cynthia Rylant, New York: Dulton.

> A special story about life in Appalachia.

Friday Night Is Papa Night (1987) by Ruth Sonnenberg, Orlan, CA: Penguin.

> Pedro can't wait for Friday night, when Papa comes home.

Songs, Movement, and Games

Songs/Movement

1. Songs from the Album *We All Live Together*

Two popular songs using the days of the week are "Everybody Loves Saturday Night" and "Days of the Week in English and Spanish." Both songs are on the album, *We All Live Together*.

2. "The Mulberry Bush"

"The Mulberry Bush" is a traditional song that combines music, movement, and the names of the days of the week. Have the children form a circle and hold hands while they sing verse 1.

Verse 1:

> Here we go 'round the mulberry bush,
> the mulberry bush, the mulberry bush.
> Here we go 'round the mulberry bush
> so early in the morning.

As they sing, they move around to the right.

For verse 2, tell the children to drop hands and dramatize washing clothes.

Verse 2:

> This is the way we wash our clothes,
> wash our clothes, wash our clothes.
> This is the way we wash our clothes
> So early Monday morning.

Have children continue to sing the verses with a new day of the week and a new action (such as eat our breakfast, go to sleep, or dress for school). Invite children to suggest actions that can be sung and dramatized.

Games

1. Hula Party

Bring in one or two Hula-Hoops (most physical education departments have Hula-Hoops available). Show the children how to hula and then show them how to use a stopwatch to time how long they can do the hula. Write the time on the chalkboard and let children try to beat their "times."

Learning Centers

Drama Center

1. "My Week" Drama

Have the children make up skits to demonstrate different actions from the "My Week" poem. Have a variety of stuffed animals or puppets available to act out and say the poem.

Writing Center

1. Digital Clocks

Children like to write numbers and words imitating the seven-segment read-out system used on digital clocks. Provide toothpicks or graph paper for this activity. Children can read the wall clock in the room and convert to a digital figure.

2. Recordkeeping

Have available copies of *What Did I Eat Today?* (see page 90). Encourage the children to use *What Did I Eat Today?* as a model for designing other recording sheets. They might record:

- How much time they spent watching TV

- What chores they did for one week

- How much time the class spends in art, gym, lunch, and at the library

---

Assessment Tip

Do not be tempted to interfere in children's attempts to create record sheets. When they try to use their record sheets to record data, they will discover their own errors and make the necessary corrections. When a child asks for help, offer suggestions. The way in which children design their record sheets will indicate their level of understanding.

- How much time they spend sleeping

- How much time is spent eating breakfast, lunch, dinner

You may want to have the children complete their record sheets as homework assignments.

3. Newspaper Work

Provide materials needed to work on the class newspaper, *Our Week in Review* (see pages 73–74).

4. Journals Continued

Provide blank books for children to continue to work on their journals or logs of the day's or week's events. To help develop appreciation for time intervals, have children focus their logs on different time spans (e.g., hourly log, center log, daily log, etc.).

5. All I Know About Time

Place chart paper in the center. Invite children to begin listing everything they know about time. At the end of each center period, allow time for the children to read their new additions and make comments.

Reading Center

1. Book Display

Place all the copies of trade books, poems, class books, and child-authored works read and developed during *Shared Reading/Writing Experiences* on display in the reading center (also see Alternate Read-Aloud Selections on pages 79–80).

2. Interesting Time Facts

Listing interesting feats and facts read about in the *Guinness Book of World Records* stimulates conversation and discussion. For example, write the following questions on chart paper:

Who spent the longest time in space? How long was that?

Who is the Hula-Hoop champion, and how long did that person twirl a single hoop?

What is the longest time spent in a rocking chair?

Provide an answer key after the children have had time to think about possible answers.

Challenge the children to create their own class records, such as reading the most books in a day or week, writing the most words in a day or week, or bouncing a ball the most times in a minute.

Math Center

1. Time Tally

Have available copies of *Time Tally* (see page 92) which allows children to track items (e.g., the number of red cars that go by a certain place, or books read, lunches bought, chocolate milk ordered) during the same period of time every day. Give children the opportunity to share what they've tallied.

Discovery Center

1. Plant a Seed

Have available three or four different seeds (e.g., bean, marigold, tomato, corn). Ask, "Which seed do you think will sprout first?" Plant on a Friday. Let the children choose the seeds to plant. Use clear containers, and plant the seed next to the side of the container so children can observe the seed grow.

Another way to plant a seed and watch growth is to place the seed on a very wet paper towel inside a self-sealing plastic bag. Tape the bag to the side of a child's desk. Label the bag with the name of the seed.

Have available the record sheet *Tracking Plant Growth* (see page 93). Explain how to use the sheet to track the sprouting of the seed.

If the seeds have been planted in pots, the children can continue to track plant growth for one or two weeks. Encourage them to use the record sheet to record the height of the plant.

2. Time Zones

Have available reference books, maps, or globes. Write the following questions on a card and post it in the center. Let the children guess the answers to the questions. Then have them research the answers. They can interview parents or the librarian, or they can refer to the reference books that are available. Note that this activity requires "reversible thought," a concrete stage of thinking and will be difficult for younger children who are preoperational thinkers.

- How many time zones are there in the United States?

- If it's 8:00 in the morning in New York, what time is it in California? Florida? Hawaii? Denver?

- From where you live, how long would it take to get to Boston, San Francisco, Denver by car? By train? By plane?

3. Sundial

On a sunny day, have the children make a sundial.

Materials needed:

- A large white piece of plastic
- A clump of clay
- A stick
- A compass

Place the plastic cloth in a sunny location. Using the compass, locate North. Write N on the cloth to mark North. Place the clay in the center of the cloth. Punch the stick through the clay and the cloth so that the stick is pushed into the ground. Children can observe the shadow and its movements throughout the day, noting lengths, pattern, and time of day. For other ideas and background information about time and sundials, read *This Book Is About Time* (1978) by Marilyn Burns.

4. Moldy Bread

Provide different kinds of bread and pose the question, "How long does it take for a piece of bread to get moldy?" Experiment using white, rye, pumpernickel, and other different kinds of bread. Try bread with and without preservatives. Have the children label each sample carefully and write about their observations in a log or on a sheet of chart paper.

Art Center

1. Painting Station

Set up a painting easel with a variety of watercolors. Children will enjoy painting or drawing a mural depicting Cookie's antics for the week.

2. Newspaper Drawings

Urge children to create then submit drawings, cartoons, and sketches for the classroom newspaper.

Sand and Water Center

1. Water Experiment

Continue the water experiments begun in the previous subtheme unit, *Sunrise to Sunset* (see pages 57–58). Use containers of different sizes and shapes.

2. Evaporation

Use rubber bands to attach a strip of paper to a plastic jar filled with colored water. Tell the children to record the daily amount of evaporation by marking the strip of paper with the day of the week. This is a perfect opportunity to demonstrate the use of abbreviations.

Cooking Experience

Instant Pudding

Show several boxes of instant pudding. Discuss what the word *instant* means. Use examples that children recognize (e.g., instant coffee, "Come here this instant"). Ask, "How long does it take to make instant pudding?" Before the children make the pudding, ask them how long they think it will take to make the pudding.

Make the pudding following the directions on the box. Time the activity. Before the children eat the pudding ask whether they agree or disagree with the use of the word *instant* in the name, *instant pudding*. Share the time it took to make. (This is also an opportunity to compare using a mixing spoon versus an egg beater. Which makes the job easier?)

On another day, make cooked pudding. Keep track of how long it takes to make. Compare the length of time it took to make both kinds of pudding. Ask children why they think the manufacturers chose the word *instant* to describe their product.

On _____

When It

_____

By _____

On _____ when it

_____ , I felt

_____ .

On _____ when it

_____ , I felt

_____ .

On _____ when it

_____ , I felt

_____ .

My Week

By _____

The End

On _____ ,

_____ .

There _____

_____ .

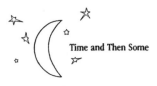
Name _____ **Date** _____

What Did I Eat Today?

	Breakfast	Lunch	Dinner	Snack
Monday				
Tuesday				
Wednesday				
Thursday				
Friday				
Saturday				
Sunday				

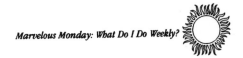

Name _____ **Date** _____

Yesterday and the Day Before

Monday   Tuesday   Wednesday   Thursday   Friday   Saturday   Sunday

Today is _____ .

Yesterday was _____ .

The day before yesterday was _____ .

Tomorrow is _____ .

Yesterday I _____ all day long.

The day before I _____ .

Today I'm going to _____ .

Tomorrow I will _____ .

Name _____ **Date** _____

Time Tally

What I'm measuring is _____ .

The time when I'll measure is _____ .

I'll measure for _____ minutes.

Monday	
Tuesday	
Wednesday	
Thursday	
Friday	

Name _____ **Date** _____

Tracking Plant Growth
_____

Circle one.

I planted a _____ .

bean   marigold   tomato   other

I planted my seed on _____ .

Monday   Tuesday   Wednesday   Thursday   Friday

My seed sprouted on _____ .

Monday   Tuesday   Wednesday   Thursday   Friday

Height After Sprouting

Day 1 _____   Day 6 _____

Day 2 _____   Day 7 _____

Day 3 _____   Day 8 _____

Day 4 _____   Day 9 _____

Day 5 _____   Day 10 _____

Full Moon:
When Is My Birthday?

Overview

One of the most exciting events in a young child's life is the child's birthday. The subtheme unit, *Full Moon*, capitalizes on this interest as a starting point for talking about the months. Shared reading experiences such as *Benjamin's 365 Birthdays* (1992) by Judi Barrett and *Chicken Soup with Rice: A Book of Months* (1962) by Maurice Sendak provide opportunities for children to share birthday stories. Making lists of birthday presents received and researching family birthdays lead to several graphing activities.

The question, "How do you know when it's your birthday?" sets the stage for inventing a classroom calendar to be used for a month. Recommended nonfiction books offer children information about the phases of the moon and how they affect our concept of time.

The *Sharing: From Invitations to Celebrations* section is stocked with a variety of activities designed to help children investigate the following questions:

How long is a month?

What are the names of the months?

How long is a year?

The Bears' Almanac: A Year in Bear Country (1973) introduces a new resource, the almanac. One follow-up activity is to write a classroom almanac based on important school events for the year.

All activities and literature in *Full Moon* are designed to provide children with an understanding of how the calendar year is composed of 12 months and that the calendar follows a predictable pattern.

Skills and Concepts

Listening/Speaking/Reading/Writing

Improve vocabulary development	Dictate and read sentences
Recall information from a story	Sequence events from a story
Compare and contrast story versions	Recite nursery rhymes or poems
Use a story map to retell a story	Read the days of the week and months
Create an innovation on a poem	Match words

Understand and use temporal concepts: yesterday, today, tomorrow, before, after,

week, month, year, season, holiday

Math

Order the days of the week	Graph information
Order the months in a year	Use a calendar
Create patterns	Count to 31
Measure with cups	

Science

Be aware of the relationships among the moon, stars, the sun, and the earth

Relate the phases of the moon to a calendar

Understand the purpose of a calendar

Compare and contrast the earth, the moon, and the sun

Understand the terms: orbit, rotate, revolve

Social Studies

Work cooperatively in a small group

Understand how ancient people told time

Understand how people use almanacs

Planning Ahead

Supplies to Gather

Colorful gift wrap, bows, and ribbons

The Print Shop (optional) software by Broderbund, Novato, CA (1-800-548-1798)

8$\frac{1}{2}$" x 11" sheets of paper

Experience chart and paper

Scissors, one per child

Yellow, green, and white
headbands or ribbon

Manipulatives for counting activities
(e.g., pebbles, cubes, colored
paper clips)

Paper clips

Construction paper (8$\frac{1}{2}$" x 11" or
11" x 17") or tagboard (17$\frac{1}{2}$" x 22")

Pocket folder

Index cards

Mural paper

Jump ropes

Old and current calendars

Sheets of paper for child illustrations
and for creating books

Sentence strips (or tagboard cut into
3" x 17" strips)

Glue or glue sticks

Flashlight

Globe

Glitter

Stapler/staples

Cooking supplies (bowl, spoon,
chocolate crisp cereal, coconut,
ground nuts, vanilla ice cream,
baking cups)

Books

Benjamin's 365 Birthdays (1992) by J. Barrett, New York: Atheneum.

The Moon Seems to Change (1987) by F. Branley, New York: Crowell.

First Explorers on the Moon. (1969). *National Geographic, 136*(6), 735–797.

Goodnight Moon (1991) by M.W. Brown, New York: Harper Collins.

Chicken Soup with Rice: A Book of Months (1962) by Maurice Sendak, New York:
Harper and Row.

Various almanacs

The Bears Almanac: A Year in Bear Country (1973) by S. Berenstain and J.
Berenstain, New York: Random House.

Rumpelstiltskin (1986) by P. Zelinsky, New York: Dutton.

Alternate versions of *Rumpelstiltskin* (see page 109)

Mooncake (1989) by F. Asch, New York: Scholastic.

Ask Mr. Bear (1986) by M. Flack, New York: Macmillan.

Various alternate read-aloud selections (see page 112)

Birthday books (see page 115)

Pages to Duplicate

I See, page 120, 1 per child

I Could Tell It Was, page 121, 4 per child, and extras for the writing center

When Is Your Birthday?, page 122, 1 per child

Calendar Page, page 123, a supply for the math center

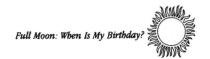

Sharing: From Invitations to Celebrations

One of the most important events of the year to a young child is his or her birthday. *Benjamin's 365 Birthdays* (1992) by Judi Barrett provides a wonderful entry into the topic of birthdays, the months, and the year.

1. Read Aloud

Read *Benjamin's 365 Birthdays*. To preserve the good feelings that accompany birthday celebrations, Benjamin decides to give himself a birthday present every day of the year.

After reading the book, discuss the idea of giving oneself a present daily. Most children will enthusiastically accept the suggestion that they choose something from their desks or from home to gift wrap. Have a supply of colorful ribbons, bows, and gift wrap available in the art center. Explain that the wrapped presents will be opened at a special class celebration.

Then, plan a party. Show the children how to design and make invitations, write thank-you notes, and plan the music, refreshments, and classroom decorations. (*The Print Shop* is a software program that young children could use to make invitations, banners, and signs for the party.) The celebration can coincide with a holiday, a calendar event such as the first day of winter, a classmate's birthday, or seasonal event—or it can be a great unbirthday party for everyone. In other words, any occasion could serve as the reason for creating a party and distributing the presents. Offer suggestions, but let the children decide.

Many of the party projects can be completed in the art and/or writing centers. Not every child has to participate in making all items. Some can make invitations while others make decorations. Hold the party as a culminating event to this subtheme unit.

2. Benjamin's Gifts

Ask children to recall the presents Benjamin received. Record them on chart paper. Reread *Benjamin's 365 Birthdays* to check for accuracy.

3. Class Birthday Gifts

Have children recall presents they have received for their birthdays and list them on chart paper as they are named. The children probably have received the same kinds of presents so graph or categorize the gifts as you list them.

Birthday Presents

Clothes	Bicycle	Book	Stuffed Animal	Game
Joan Sue Johnny	Joan		Joan Sue	Johnny

4. When Is My Birthday?

Find and mark Benjamin's birthday on a calendar. Mark the birthdays of all the children on the calendar. Ask, "How do you know when it's your birthday?" Write facts on the chalkboard as you discuss these questions:

- What would it be like if we didn't have any way of telling which day it is?

- How did people tell time and predict events without the calendar?

- What did ancient people use?

How Did People Tell Time?
Counting days (suns)
Counting sunrises and sunsets
Looking at the moon
Counting number of harvests
Watching the stars
and constellations

Lead the discussion to these facts: Ancient people watched the stars, the sun, and the moon. They observed that the stars, sun, and moon move in predictable patterns. The moon's appearance changes over a period of every 28 to $29\frac{1}{2}$ days from a new moon to a full moon. These regular changes became known as the months. The word *month* comes from the word *moon*. Ask, "Does the moon always look the same to us?"

To determine the children's prior knowledge, ask them to draw a picture of what the moon looks like to them. Have each child cut out their moons and tack them on a bulletin board.

The Moon

1. Read Aloud

Read *The Moon Seems to Change* (1960) by Franklyn Branley and Helen Borten. Referring to the children's pictures of the moon, discuss which pictures are correct, and why.

Reread *The Moon Seems To Change*. List ways in which the moon is different from Earth. Discuss how we know what the moon is like. Children will exhibit varying amounts of knowledge about the moon. This is an opportunity for them to share information with their classmates. Suggest that they bring to school and share pictures, toys, and tapes about the moon. Display pictures of the moon landing from the 1969 *National Geographic* article "First Explorers on the Moon."

2. Drama of Moon's Cycle

Use dramatic play to explain the meanings of the words *orbit, rotate,* and *revolve.* Have four or five children hold hands and form a circle, with their backs to the center of the circle. Give each child a yellow headband or ribbon to designate them as the sun. Choose two children to wear green headbands or ribbons and hold hands facing each other, portraying Earth. Have another child wearing a white headband or ribbon be the moon.

Tell the sun to stand still. While the moon moves (*revolves*) around Earth, direct Earth to rotate as it moves (*revolves*) around the sun. Each stays within its own orbit.

Periodically, stop the action and question the two Earth people individually ("Can you see the sun? Can you see the moon? Is it day or night?"). Let the children who are role-playing choose classmates to take their places until all have had an opportunity to take part.

The Calendar

1. How Many Days?

Ask, "What do we use to help us know when to celebrate our birthdays, holidays, and other events?" List the children's responses on chart paper. Ask questions such as: "What is a month?" and "How long is a month?"

Ask the children to estimate how many sheets of paper are equal to the number of the days in a month. (If the children tracked one week as suggested in the previous subtheme unit, *Marvelous Monday*, probably they will realize that a month represents a longer period.) Record their answers.

After children's responses are recorded, hang 30 sheets of 8¹/₂" x 11" paper one by one. Invite children to count with you as you hang the sheets around the room. Explain that each sheet represents one day in a month, so most months are 30 days long.

Invite children to suggest ways the 30 sheets can be arranged and named so they can be used as a calendar for the class. Tell the children, "There are 30 days in a month and we have 30 sheets of paper. We can use the sheets of paper to make a calendar, but all the sheets of paper look the same. We have to think of a way we can mark them so each sheet looks different." Present a problem: "Pretend that you are invited to a friend's birthday party on the 26th day of the month. You want to record the date so you won't miss the party. Who can think of a way to mark the sheets so they can be used to help us remember this important day?" Accept and list children's suggestions. Some ideas children may offer are:

- Mark each sheet with a different color crayon

- Mark each sheet with a letter

- Use numbers

- Use different shapes

Discuss and demonstrate each idea. For instance, if a child suggests marking each sheet with a different color crayon, it will become apparent quickly that 30 colors are needed. If you have the time, give children a chance to explore the various ideas suggested by giving them a packet of 30 sheets. Let the children work in pairs or in small groups and provide time for them to share their discoveries.

Based on prior experiences, children probably will realize that numbers and the names of the days of the week work best for organizing the calendars. Ask children to help you organize the 30 sheets. Show them how you repeat the days of the week to create four weeks. Compare your class calendar with a commercial calendar. Count the number of days in the various months and tell the children that some months have 31 days and one has 28 (or 29) days.

Even though the sheets of paper take up a lot of room, use them as the calendar for the current month. Record the name of the month and special events that will occur during that period (special classroom events, holidays, birthdays, and other days that are special for individual children). This activity may take several days to accomplish.

Assessment Tip

This group activity will demonstrate children's understanding of the mechanics of the calendar. For many children, the activity will help them to understand how the days of the week fit into the calendar and to recognize the repetitive pattern used in the calendar system.

---

2. Daily Calendar Routines

Practice calendar routines daily. Ask, "If today is Monday, what day was it yesterday?" and "What day will it be tomorrow?" Use manipulatives (pebbles, cubes, colored paper clips, and others) for counting activities. For example, if the children are counting the number of days in each week, place manipulatives in front of the children as they name and count the days.

Mark special events on the calendar—birthdays, holidays, field trips, and other events. Make a paper-clip chain with each clip representing one day. Every day, mark off or count how many days remain until the event. Ask the children to count how many days are left and remove one paper clip each day. The children will see the chain getting shorter and shorter. Every day, record the number of days left.

3. Class Calendar

For each new month, make a calendar with the class. Have the children say and spell the days of the week as you write them, and have them count the days as you write the numbers (or whenever possible, invite children to do the recording or writing of numbers). On the first day of each month, select a manipulative to use for counting off each day. For example, place a pebble in a container to represent one day. Count the number of pebbles in the container every day. Record the number of days on the chalkboard or on calculator tape.

Ask, "Does every month have 30 days?" Look at a calendar and list on chart paper the names of the months that have 30 days, 31 days, and 28 (or 29) days.

Shared Reading/Writing Experiences

Poems

1. Read Aloud

Write the following poem, "Thirty Days Has September" on large chart paper. Hang it in a prominent place and have the children chant it daily.

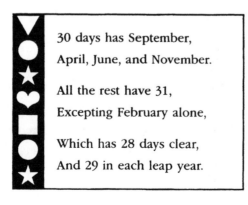

> 30 days has September,
> April, June, and November.
>
> All the rest have 31,
> Excepting February alone,
>
> Which has 28 days clear,
> And 29 in each leap year.

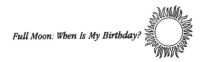

Moon Poems

1. Read Aloud

Write the following poems, "Hey, Diddle, Diddle" and "I See the Moon" on large chart paper. Read them every day.

> **Hey, Diddle, Diddle**
>
> Hey, diddle, diddle.
> The cat and the fiddle.
> The cow jumped over the moon.
> The little dog laughed to see such sport,
> And the dish ran away with the spoon.
>
> **I See the Moon**
>
> I see the moon,
> And the moon sees me.
> "Hello, moon."
> "Hello, me."

2. I See

When the children are very familiar with the poem "I See the Moon," ask them to substitute words for *the moon*. For example:

> I see *a bird*
> And *the bird* sees me.
> "Hello, *bird*."
> "Hello, me."

Distribute the *I See* page (see page 120) to each child and have the children write their substitutions and then draw them on the *I See* page. Create a title page for an *I See the Moon* class book. Bind the children's innovations with the title page to form the class book. Read the book daily for a while, then place the book in the reading center.

Goodnight Moon

1. Read Aloud

Read *Goodnight, Moon* (1974) by Margaret Wise Brown. Discuss getting ready for bed and going to bed. Ask, "Do you ever try to delay bedtime?" Reread the book. Have one child keep a tally of the number of times the word *goodnight* appears in the text, then share that number with the class.

2. *Goodnight Moon* Big Book

Write the text and format of *Goodnight Moon* on large construction paper or tagboard for the purpose of making a Big Book. Have the children illustrate the Big Book by drawing the part they like best on a separate piece of paper, cutting it out, and pasting it on the appropriate page. Keep the Big Book in the reading center for all to enjoy.

Chicken Soup with Rice

1. Read Aloud

In *Chicken Soup with Rice: A Book of Months* (1962), the author, Maurice Sendak, uses humor and rhyme to lead children through the months of the year. This book will become a favorite. Within two to three pages of the first reading, children will discover the repetitive refrain and will want to read along. Read the book aloud.

Reread *Chicken Soup with Rice* and invite the children to read along. Children enjoy reading the refrain in each verse using different voices—loud and soft, high and low.

2. Birth Months

Write the verses for each month on 8¹/₂" x 11" sheets of paper. Duplicate and give the children copies of the verses that name their birth months. Organize the children to read the verses for their months from *Chicken Soup with Rice* in the order of the calendar year. They may want to take home copies of their verses to share with parents.

3. Month of Birthday Order

Arrange the children by month of birthday in a line using the same order of the months found in *Chicken Soup with Rice*. If no one has a birthday in one or two of the months named, place an index card with the name of the month written on it where a child would stand. Count the number of months. Have the children name the months.

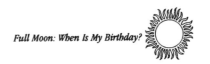

4. Months in Order

Have 12 children form a circle. Give each child an index card with the name of a month written on it. Tell the children to stand in the order that the months come in one year. Display a calendar and read the name of the months aloud. Tell the children that every year, the months are repeated in the same order. Then ask the child holding the card of the month that is *after* March to hold his or her card high. Repeat with the month *before* March. Continue this procedure asking "before" and "after" questions.

5. Earth's Rotation

Use a flashlight and a globe to demonstrate how Earth revolves around the sun. Lead children to understand that it takes the Earth 12 months to go around once.

Encourage the children to role-play Earth's journey. Have the children stand in a circle to represent the sun. Tell one child labeled Earth to move slowly around the sun. Have the children chant the names of the months as Earth revolves around the sun.

6. Body Birthday Graph

Create a "body birthday graph." Ask children to stand in a line behind the index card that names the month in which they were born. Have children count the number of people standing in each line and remind them that the number of people standing in each line tells how many people are celebrating birthdays in that month.

Use this information to make a picture graph. On a large sheet of chart paper draw 12 birthday cakes labeled with the name of a month. Have children write their names below the cake that shows the month in which they were born. Relate the picture graph to the body birthday graph created when they stood in lines.

The Bears' Almanac: A Year in Bear Country

1. Read Aloud

Tell children, "An almanac is a book that is published each year. It offers readers up-to-date information." Show children several editions of adult almanacs from several different years. Share some of the kinds of information that the almanac provides.

Read the title and the title page of *The Bears' Almanac* (1973) by Stan and Jan Berenstain. Ask children to predict the kind of information *The Bears' Almanac* provides. Read *The Bears' Almanac* in sections. (Each section relates

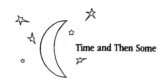
information about one season.) Take the time to talk about and share the information provided.

After each reading, have children work alone, in pairs, or in small groups (three to five children) to write about, list, or draw characteristics of that season. Have each group select one child to share the work of the group with the whole class.

2. Seasonal Words

The Bears' Almanac begins with winter and names the three winter months. When this section is complete, help the children list winter words on chart paper. When several words have been listed, hang the *Winter Words* chart in the writing center. Suggest to the children that they continue to add words as they think of them. Do this with each season.

3. I Could Tell Poems

Encourage the children to write little season poems using this model:

I could tell it was fall because:

- On Monday, I saw one red leaf falling to the ground.

- On Tuesday, I saw two big, bright orange pumpkins.

- On Wednesday, I saw three turtles burrowing in the mud.

- On Thursday, I saw four red birds flying south.

- On Friday, I saw five rabbits filling their stomachs for winter.

- On Saturday, I saw six squirrels collecting acorns and putting them in a hollow tree.

- On Sunday, I saw seven muscular football players.

Distribute *I Could Tell It Was* (see page 121) to each child and tell the children to follow your model by writing what they see in each season. Encourage the children to write a poem for each of the seasons. Keep a supply of *I Could Tell It Was* in the writing center.

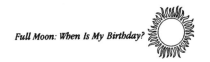

4. Holidays

In *The Bears' Almanac*, one major holiday for each season is illustrated. Have children name other holidays and illustrate them on 8½" x 11" paper. Have children find out in which month and season the holiday occurs. Exhibit the completed illustrations under seasonal categories listed on the bulletin board.

5. Classroom Almanac

Create a classroom almanac. Have the children decide what information is relevant to include in their almanac. The seasonal format used in *The Bears' Almanac* is a good format for children to model. Identifying important school events for the year is another good starting point. For example, a field trip is an event children look forward to and enjoy. The almanac might provide the date as well as background information about the event.

Rumpelstiltskin

1. Read Aloud

Rumpelstiltskin is one of the most popular of the Grimm's fairy tales. There are many versions and any one of them can be used. In *Rumpelstiltskin* (1986) retold and illustrated by Paul O. Zelinsky, beautiful oil paintings provide a splendid background for this traditional tale that takes one year to unfold. Other versions include *Rumpelstiltskin* (1973) retold by Edith Tarcow, and "Tom Tit Tom" (1976), a version included in *The Anthology of Children's Literature* edited by May Hill Arbuthnot.

2. Alternate Versions

Read and reread several versions of *Rumpelstiltskin* aloud. Ask the children which is their favorite version. Create a graph based on children's selections using cubes or some other manipulative. Designate a different color to represent each book. For example, a red cube might represent Zelensky's version and a blue cube could represent the Tarcow version. Children select their favorite book by placing one cube in front of the book they like best. When all children have had a chance to indicate their choices, stack or count the cubes to find out which version of *Rumpelstiltskin* received the most cubes.

3. Rhyming Verse

On large chart paper, write the rhyming verse sung by Rumpelstiltskin. Children will enjoy chanting this verse as if they were Rumpelstiltskin. Point out the rhyming words. Hang the chart in the drama center where children can practice reading it.

In each version, Rumpelstiltskin chants a different verse. Write all of the versions of the verses so children can see the differences.

Mooncake

1. Read Aloud

In the book *Mooncake* (1989) by Frank Asch, Bear decides the moon looks delicious enough to eat, but his friend, Little Bird, suggests that perhaps the moon tastes terrible. Bear works all summer long to build a rocket for a trip to the moon. Children will immediately recognize the gullibility of both characters. Read *Mooncake* several times. Tape a large sheet of mural paper to a chalkboard or bulletin board. First, ask children to name the events they remember. Then ask children to identify in which season the action occurred. Write the events as children name them, placing them into a seasonal framework. Completing this task may require returning to the text to find seasonal clues.

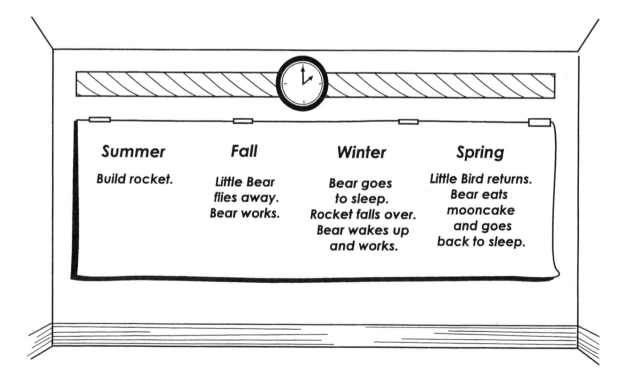

2. Months and Seasons

Have children recall the names of the months in each season. If they are unsure or have forgotten, review *The Bears' Almanac*.

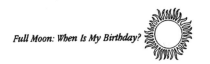

Ask Mr. Bear

1. Read Aloud

Ask Mr. Bear (1986) by Marjorie Flack is an all-time favorite with young children. Little Danny wants a special present for his mother's birthday. None of his animal friends can help him except Mr. Bear. Read the title of the book. Then read the first few sentences in *Ask Mr. Bear*. Reread the title, and ask the children what they think the book is about.

Continue to read until Danny meets Mr. Bear. Ask children to guess what Mr. Bear whispers in Danny's ear. Children will love the surprise ending.

2. Story Map

Read *Ask Mr. Bear* again. Help the children create a story map of *Ask Mr. Bear* on a large sheet of mural paper. Begin by listing all the animals Danny meets on chart paper. Have the children recall the sequence in which Danny meets the animals. Place a number next to each animal's name to indicate the correct sequence.

Then, decide with the children where to begin Danny's trip around the farm. Consult with the children as to where you should begin to draw simple pictures to illustrate where Danny went and with whom he spoke. Refer to the chart paper when needed.

When the drawings are finished, ask the children to tell the animal sound that was made by each of the animals. Add these sounds to the numbered list. Hang the large story map in the reading center along with the animal listing. At the reading center, invite children to write the animal sound on the story map in a dialogue bubble next to the appropriate animal.

Note that developing a story map demands a high degree of understanding and recall. Even though the map may not appear perfect, remember that the process is more important than the finished map.

3. When Is Your Birthday?

For homework, ask children to find out and record when family members celebrate their birthdays. Distribute *When Is Your Birthday?* (see page 122) to take home to complete. Have children share the results in a whole-group discussion.

Alternate Read-Aloud Selections

Owl Moon (1987) by Jane Yolen, New York: Putnam.

> Father and daughter walk through the snow on a cold night to catch sight of an owl.

"The Songs of the Jellicles" (1987) by T.S. Eliot, from *Cat Poems*, New York: Holiday.

> This poem is about cats at night.

The Month Brothers (1983) by Samuel Marshak, New York: Morrow.

> This beautiful Slavic fairy tale tells about a young girl whose wicked stepmother forces her to go into the woods to find spring flowers in the middle of the winter. In the frozen forest, she receives help from the 12 brothers, the months of the year.

Anansi, The Spider (1972) by Gerald McDermott, Cambridge, MA: Holt.

> In this traditional tale from the Ashanti of West Africa, Anansi, the spider, meets trouble on his long journey. His six sons save his life. To reward their efforts, Anansi gives them the moon.

Fox's Dream (1987) by Keizaburo Tejima, New York: Putnam.

> In this exquisitely illustrated book, readers follow a lonely and hungry fox through the night.

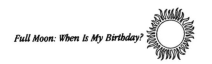

Songs, Movement, and Games

Movement

The following jump rope chants are an enjoyable outdoor or indoor gym activity.

1. Under the Sun and over the Moon

The jump rope is held taut by two children who chant the verse:

Under the sun, rope high.

Over the moon, rope low.

When the children say, "Under," the rope is held high and a child runs under the rope. When they hold the rope low and say, "Over," a child jumps over the rope.

2. All in Together

In this jump rope activity, two children steadily turn the rope while one child jumps in the center. All three children chant:

All in together,

No matter what the weather.

I spy Jack,

Peeping through the crack.

One, two, three,

Busy, busy bee.

Nineteen, twenty,

I've got plenty.

January, February, March, April,

May, June, July, August,

September, October,

November, December

Now try to remember.

We're all in together.

When the jumping child's birthday month is named, the child jumps out. Children take turns turning the rope and jumping.

If the children are not able to jump rope, have them stand in a circle, chant the verse, and clap rhythmically. When a child's birth month is named the child should sit down.

3. Each, Peach, Pear, Plum

Two children steadily turn the rope while the third child jumps rope. They all chant:

Each, peach, pear, plum.

When does your birthday come?

In this chant, the jumping child names the month and date of his or her birthday, and then all children spell the month and count the number of days. The child jumps out when the birthdate is reached.

Child: April fourth.

All: A-P-R-I-L, one, two, three, four.

For expert jump ropers, spelling and counting are done at a much quicker pace, called "Hot pepper, peach, pear, plum!"

If the children are not able to jump rope, they can sit in a circle, chant, and clap the refrain. Going around the circle, the children take turns saying their birthdays. Children hold up index cards on which their birthdays are printed so all children can see the dates and spell in unison.

Learning Centers

By this time, plans for the class party are nearly completed and children can be working on the preparations in the art and writing centers.

Drama Center

1. *Rumpelstiltskin* Drama

Rumpelstiltskin is an excellent selection for children to dramatize. Leave copies of the various versions of this story in the drama center for easy reference. Also post the chart paper with the rhyming verse sung by Rumpelstiltskin (see page 109) so children can read it while they dramatize the story and pretend to be Rumpelstiltskin.

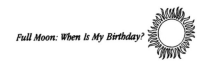

2. *Ask Mr. Bear* Drama

Leave copies of *Ask Mr. Bear* in the drama center for children to dramatize. To help children remember the various parts in *Ask Mr. Bear*, make sentence strips for each animal character and leave them in the drama center.

3. Earth's Trip

Encourage children to role-play the Earth's trip around the sun, chanting the names of the months as they travel. Display the names of the months in a prominent place.

Writing Center

1. Season Words

Display the seasonal words charts created earlier (see page 108). Invite the children to add more words as they think of them.

2. Party Designs

Designing and writing party invitations, thank-you notes, banners, signs, and posters will keep children actively engaged in this center. If possible, have a software program and computer available to help design these items.

3. Season Poem

Have available extra copies of *I Could Tell It Was* (see page 121). Encourage children to write seasonal poems using the activity page.

Reading Center

1. Book Display

Display birthday books, the various versions of *Rumpelstiltskin*, a copy of *The Bears' Almanac*, and a copy of an adult almanac. Also provide copies of other books shared in this unit. Examples of birthday books are:

A Birthday for Frances (1976) by Russel Hoban, New York: Harper.

Happy Birthday to You! (1987) by Dr. Seuss, New York: Random House.

The Secret Birthday Message (1972) by Eric Carle, New York: Harper.

Lyle and the Birthday Party (1966) by B. Warber, Boston: Houghton Mifflin.

Corduroy's Party (1977) by Don Freeman, New York: Penguin.

Birthday Poems (1989) by Myra Cohn Livingston, New York: Holiday.

Ask Mr. Bear (1986) by Marjorie Flack, New York: Macmillan.

2. *I See the Moon* Class Book

Display the class-authored book titled *I See the Moon* for children to read.

3. *Goodnight Moon* Big Book

Display the *Goodnight Moon* Big Book created by the children. Encourage children to read this class-authored book.

4. Chart of Verses

Have available copies of the verses from *Chicken Soup with Rice*. Have the children practice reading from the verses.

The verses also can be used for a matching activity. On index cards, write words from the verses. Store the cards in a pocket folder by the chart. Tell children to select cards from the folder and match them to words on the chart.

5. Story Map

Display the story map for *Ask Mr. Bear* which children began earlier (see page 111). Children can write the different sounds made by animals in dialogue bubbles next to each animal. Also display the chart of animals and animal sounds listed previously (see pages 111–112).

Ask children to make their own story maps of *Ask Mr. Bear*, or use any other story to create a story map.

6. Three Events

Fold sheets of paper to make three sections. Have a supply of these papers available in the center. Tell children to draw the three most important events from *Rumpelstiltskin*.

Math Center

1. Calendar Puzzle

Disassemble an old calendar. Cut off the names of all the months except January. Challenge children to reassemble the calendar in the correct order. Children might use calendar clues such as holidays to reassemble the calendar.

2. Make a Calendar

Have children make their own calendars. Provide a supply of the blank *Calendar Page* (see page 123) which has only the days of the week printed on the top. Tell children to fill in the numbers and the name of the month. (Have a current calendar available for reference.)

3. Calendar Count

Have several outdated calendars, a supply of blank chart paper, and marking pens available in the center. Invite children to write the names of the month on the chart paper. Then count and record the number of days in each month.

January	February	March	April	May	June
		31 days			30 days
July	August	September	October	November	December
31 days 29 days					

Sometimes there will be a discrepancy; for instance, in the example above, one child wrote that July has 31 days and another child recorded 29 days. When a discrepancy occurs have children repeat the counting and cross out the incorrect count.

4. Patterns

Time is based on the patterns found in nature. The clock follows a pattern. The following activities help to develop children's awareness and appreciation for patterning. Demonstrate each activity, then ask children to record their patterns on a sheet of paper so that other children can reproduce the original patterns. When demonstrating patterns, show children that a pattern can continue repeating endlessly. An excellent resource for patterning activities is Chapter 2 of *Math Their Way* (1976) by Mary Barrata Lorton, Reading, MA: Addison-Wesley. Activities suggested include:

- Build pattern block walls.
- Make trains from cubes with patterned colors.
- Use leaves, rocks, seeds, keys, buttons, and other materials to form a pattern.
- Arrange colored paper clips in a pattern.

Discovery Center

1. Earth's Orbit

Have a flashlight and a globe available for children to demonstrate the Earth's travels around the sun.

2. Moon/Sun Videos

Have videotapes about the moon and the sun available in the center for children to view.

3. Moon Observations

Invite children to observe the phases of the moon. Then have them record the date and their sightings on index cards. Display the cards for children to read and compare.

4. Unique Calendars

Challenge the children to create their own unique calendars by inventing different days and months.

Art Center

1. Story Mural

Children paint a mural based on any of the books shared, to serve as a backdrop for the drama center.

2. Holiday Art

Tell children to draw or paint pictures depicting a special holiday celebrated annually.

3. Gift Wrap Center

Have available gift wrap, colorful ribbons and bows, and tape for children to wrap gifts for themselves (see the *Read Aloud* activity on page 99). The children can open the gifts during the celebration described.

4. Party Hats

Invite children to make party hats. To make a party hat, children should cut a 4" x 18" strip of construction paper and decorate it with glitter and paper scraps. Then measure the paper strip to fit around his or her head and staple. Tell the children to tear or cut the top edge to create a crown effect.

5. Party Decorations

Have available supplies to make posters and paper chains to decorate the classroom. To make paper chains, have children work in the small center group to cut construction paper (in assorted colors) into 1$\frac{1}{2}$" x 7" strips. Show them how to fold a strip, interlock it with another strip, and apply glue along the edges to form a small ring. Have the center group hang their decorations.

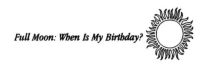

Sand and Water Center

1. Story Map

In the sandbox, tell children to recreate the story map of *Ask Mr. Bear*. Provide farm animal props and figurines to add interest to this activity.

2. Earth's Orbit

Show the children how they can draw a diagram in the sand of how the Earth revolves around the sun.

Cooking Experience

Moon Cake

1 cup chocolate crisp cereal

2 cups coconut

$\frac{1}{2}$ cup ground nuts or nut topping

vanilla ice cream

paper baking cups

Mix dry ingredients in a bowl. Quickly roll one scoop of ice cream in dry mixture. Place in a paper baking cup. Freeze until ready to eat.

Name _____ **Date** _____

I See

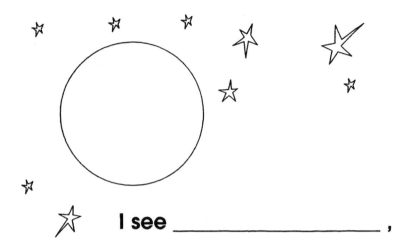

I see _____ ,

And _____ sees me.

"Hello, _____."

"Hello, me."

Name _____ Date _____

I Could Tell It Was

I could tell it was _____ because:

On Monday, I saw one _____.

On Tuesday, I saw two _____.

On Wednesday, I saw three _____.

On Thursday, I saw four _____.

On Friday, I saw five _____.

On Saturday, I saw six _____.

On Sunday, I saw seven _____.

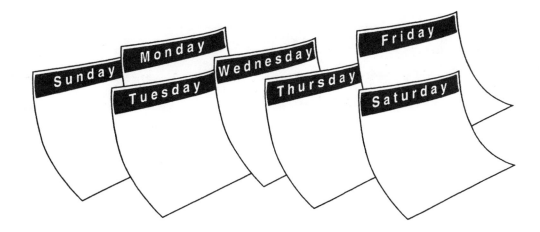

Name _____ **Date** _____

When Is Your Birthday?

Ask the members of your family, "In what month is your birthday?"
Write their names next to the names of the months.

	Family Birthdays
January	
February	
March	
April	
May	
June	
July	
August	
September	
October	
November	
December	

Calendar Page

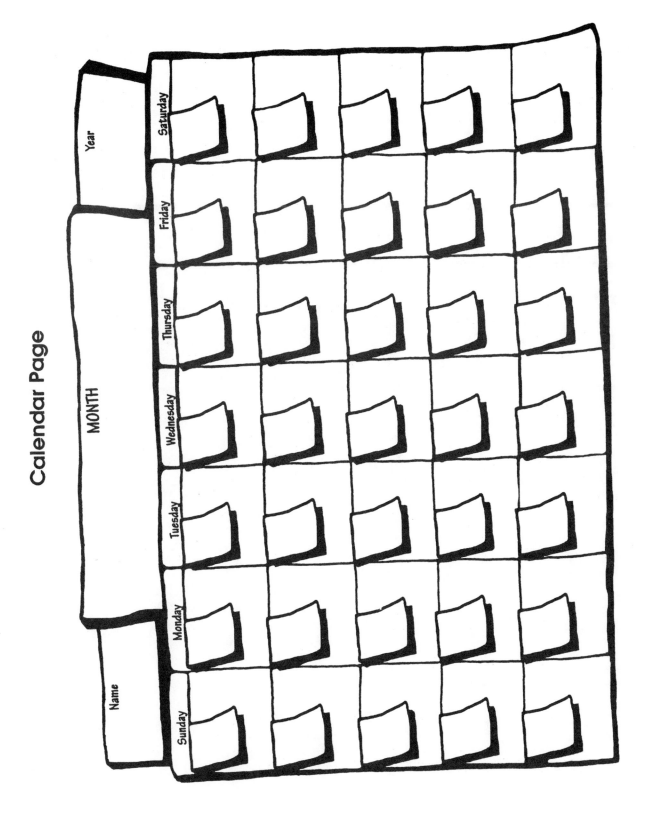

Name

MONTH

Year

Sunday	Monday	Tuesday	Wednesday	Thursday	Friday	Saturday

Good Times:
What Are My Favorite Days?

Overview

Begin the subtheme unit, *Good Times*, by asking children to think about the special days they experience throughout the year. Children's discussions provide a wonderful opportunity to share unique family and cultural traditions. The Good Times Parade is a culminating event designed to bring closure to the unit. The parade also serves as a medium for celebrating student diversity.

Experience charts, class books, and student projects developed through the unit are reviewed and then put on display. Parents, friends, and school personnel are invited to view the artifacts and to enjoy the Good Times Parade.

In this subtheme unit, children are involved in problem-solving activities using very large numbers. After reading *How Much Is a Million?* (1994) by David Schwartz, children are challenged to think and talk about counting to a million. Can children count and collect a million bottle caps? Probably not—but they'll have a lot of fun trying.

Children will learn about the special days that occur annually, special days in nature, and special days that are celebrated in a country.

Skills and Concepts

Listening/Speaking/Reading/Writing

Identify special days/holidays in a year	Categorize special days
List items alphabetically	Write upper-case and lower-case
Describe thought and observations in	alphabet letters
complete sentences	Listen attentively to readings

Dictate and read sentences

Segment words into sounds

Create an innovation of a poem

Rhyme words

Recognize the purpose of quotation
 marks

Understand and use time concepts:
 year, annual, days in a year,
 months in a year, seasons in a year

Sequence events from a story

Match text

Math

Use a calendar to mark special days
 and changes of seasons

Count to 365

Recognize patterns in large numbers

Count backwards

Understand the size of a million

Estimate time

Science

Understand the relationship of the
 Earth and sun to the duration
 of a year

Keep time to music

Categorize activities and environmental
 changes by season

Compare/contrast seasons

Order the seasons of the year

Social Studies

Plan a parade

Work cooperatively in small groups

Planning Ahead

Supplies to Gather

Camera and film

Red and blue markers

Scrapbook or three-ring binder,
 one per child

8½" x 11" sheets of paper

Large paper clips, 12 boxes

Calendars

Pencils, 12

Experience chart and paper

Pocket folders

Plastic bags for counting activity

Paper bags

Costumes for the drama center (see
 page 143)

Old magazines or photos

Mural paper

Watercolor paints

Globe

Sentence strips (or tagboard cut into 3" x 17" strips and 3" x 8½" strips)

4" x 6" index cards

Large manila envelopes

Rhythm instruments (e.g., tambourines triangles, sticks, blocks, bells, drums)

Stick pins

Paper plates

Manipulatives for counting (e.g., beans, paper clips, pebbles)

Flashlight

Scissors

Cross-section of tree or branch showing growth rings

Toy boats

Popsicle sticks

Books

Now We Are Six (1955) by A.A. Milne, New York: Dutton.

Several ABC books (see page 129–130)

Cookbooks for young children

How Much Is a Million? (1994) by D.M. Schwartz, New York: Mulberry.

Various books dealing with large numbers (see page 136)

Almanac

The Berenstain Bears' Almanac: A Year in Bear Country (1973) by J. and S. Berenstain, New York: Random House.

Various alternate read-aloud selections (see page 141)

Pages to Duplicate

My Special Days, page 148, one per child and extra copies for the reading center

January Snow, page 149, one per child

Seasons Poem, page 150, two per child and extras for the writing center

Instrument Symbols, page 151, several copies to create cards and extra copies for the discovery center

Owl and *Pussy-Cat Masks*, pages 152–153, copies for the drama center

Cooking Through the Year, page 154, one copy per child

Sharing: From Invitations to Celebrations

1. Growing Up Year by Year

Take an individual photograph of each child. On the backs of the photos, have children write their names, ages, and the date. Ask children to bring in four to six photographs from home that show them at different ages. These photographs can be shared in several ways. Talk about how each year they have changed.

- Display the photos on the bulletin board. Read Alan Alexander Milne's poem, "The End," from *Now We Are Six* (1955). Place an enlarged copy of the poem next to the display.

- Have the children make a Big Book for presenting the photographs.

- Invite children to create individual books by pasting their pictures into blank books. They can name their books and label each photo. If they choose, they can write something about themselves under each photograph They can dedicate their books to their parents or someone equally special. These books make excellent gifts for Mother's Day, Father's Day, or Grandparents' Day. Photographs can be reproduced on most photocopiers or scanned on a computer. Make many copies of the photographs. Paste them on the covers of books authored by the children. Encourage children to write short biographical sketches to accompany their photographs.

2. My Special Days

Help children name an approaching special day appropriate for presenting their books to someone special. As children begin naming special days, record them on chart paper. Display the list in a prominent place. Return to the list on several occasions to continue adding special days. Lead children to name important days including holidays. Continue adding to the list until children stop volunteering suggestions.

Read the final list and have children identify only the special school days (e.g., (end of year picnic). Circle those days with a red marker. Use a blue marker to identify special seasonal days (e.g., Memorial Day).

Distribute a copy of *My Special Days* (see page 148) to each child. Explain to the children that they should continue to separate the days on the list into the categories written on the activity page. Children can work in pairs or in small groups to complete this activity.

Have the children take the activity page home to share with their families. Suggest that they ask someone at home to help them use a calendar to find the dates of the days on their activity pages.

Special Days

Hanukkah	Super Bowl
Father's Day	Pet Show
Book Fair	Field Day
Christmas	The day the pool opens
Ramadan	First day of hunting
July 4th	Little League opening
Birthday	Summer festival
Ballet Recital	Summer vacation begins

3. ABC Book of Special Days

Begin an *ABC Book of Special Days*, using a scrapbook or a three-ring binder with 27 blank pages (one page for the title page). Read several ABC books. Then ask the children to write and illustrate their own books based on the alphabet. Help the children write an upper-case and lower-case letter at the  top corner of each page in their books in alphabetical order. Place their books in the writing center. Invite children to glue photos, magazine pictures, or drawings of holidays in the book, arranging the items by the initial consonant of the holiday.

Example ABC Books:

Eating the Alphabet: Fruits and Vegetables from A to Z (1989) by Lois Ehlert, San Diego, CA: Harcourt, Brace, Jovanovich.

C Is for Curious: An ABC of Feelings (1990) by Woodleigh Hubbard, San Francisco, CA: Chronicle Books.

Animalia (1987) by Graeme Base, New York: Abrams.

The Handmade Alphabet (1991) by Laura Rankin, New York: Dial Books.

To maintain student interest in the project, allow time for the children to show what they have pasted into their books. The book will take time to develop. Give positive reinforcement and routinely remind the children to add to the book. When the book is completed, ask children for suggestions on how to present their books to friends, parents, the principal, and others.

4. What We've Learned

At this point in the unit, children realize that time follows a pattern based on natural events and daily activities. To illustrate this point and to refresh the children's memories, focus their attention on the many charts developed during the last few weeks.

Experience charts created in activities in other subtheme units:

Daytime/Nighttime (page 33)

The Days of the Week (page 72)

Every Day (daily)/Once a Week (weekly) chart in *Daily/Weekly Journals* (page 73)

Seasonal Words (page 108)

Use this occasion to talk about what the children have learned about time. Record their statements.

5. Annual Events

Ask children to list or write about the events they expect to take place every year. Allow children a few days to complete the list so they have time to discuss the subject with family and friends.

Things that Happen Every Year
Birthday
Going to School
Snow
Summer
Going to Camp
Daddy grows a garden
Book Fair
Family reunion

Assessment Tip

Lists can be used to assess children's understanding of the duration of a year and the annual events that occur.

---

6. How Long Is a Year?

Have the following materials available:

12 boxes of large paper clips

12 calendar pages, each showing a month of the year

12 sheets of paper

12 pencils

Ask the children, "How long is a year? How many days are in a year?" Write their responses on the chalkboard. Then have children form lines according to their birthday months. When children are in place, have them sit on the floor, staying together in small groups representing their birthday months. Spread the groups around the room.

Assign the following jobs to members of each group (for groups smaller than four, assign more than one job to group members):

Materials person: Gets materials and returns them

Counter: Places manipulatives on a calendar page

Recorder: Writes the number of paper clips used in this exercise

Reporter: Reports to the whole class the number of paper clips used

Have the materials person get the materials (i.e., box of paper clips, calendar page of the appropriate month, one sheet of paper, one pencil) and bring them to the group.

Instruct the children to count the number of days in their assigned month.

While they count, one child (the counter) places a paper clip on the square representing each day.

When the children have finished counting, tell the counter to connect the paper clips and the recorder to write

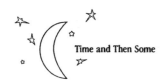

the number of paper clips on a sheet of paper. Ask the reporters to announce to the class the number of paper clips in that month.

If no children have birthdays in a particular month, prepare the paper clips in advance, or ask children to do it for you.

Have the children come together as a class. Say the names of the month with the children. Connect all the paper clips that represent each month. Ask the children to first think about, then tell, what period of time all the paper clips represent. Expect some silly answers ("A day"; "A month"; "Forever").

Eventually, one of the children will guess or realize that the paper clips represent one year. When this happens (or if you decide to give them this information), ask children how many paper clips are connected. Record the children's estimates on the chalkboard.

With the children, count the number of paper clips. Compare their estimates to the accurate count. Ask them to tell whether their estimate was more or less than 365.

This activity may take a few days to complete but do not be tempted to rush. Allow time for the children to get involved and reflect upon the activities.

7. Good Times Parade

Plan a parade of special days with the children. Name the parade the "Good Times Parade." Explain that a parade is an activity designed to involve a lot of people celebrating a special event. The Good Times Parade will be the class's way to celebrate the end of the unit in which they have learned so much about time and had such a good time.

This parade can be very elaborate or simple, depending on time and energy available. Preparations for the parade can be completed in the learning centers.

Involve the children in planning for the Good Times Parade. With the children, pick a date for the parade and mark this event on the classroom calendar. Refer to the calendar daily, counting backward to this culminating event.

Assessment Tip

Counting backward is a basic subtraction activity. Ask the children to calculate how many days are left until the parade. Have them record the number on a scrap piece of paper. Ask them to hold up their answers. This will allow you to identify at a glance any children who have difficulty with this concept.

Help the children discuss and make plans for:

Refreshments

Classroom decorations (holiday banners and posters representing holidays and special days)

Music

Guest list (special invitations to be made at the art center and writing center)

Costumes (representing annual holidays and other special days)

As the children make suggestions, record them on chart paper and tack them to a wall.

Be sure to hold the Good Times Parade at the end of this unit. Remember to display charts, class- and child-authored books, and projects created during the entire time unit.

Date	Guest List	Refreshments
March 1	Moms Dads Grandmas Grandpas Principal	popcorn juice

Costumes	Decorations	Music
ballet costume little league shirt Halloween mask	banner posters	rhythm instruments "The Syncopated Clock"

Shared Reading/Writing Experiences

How Much Is a Million?

How Much Is a Million? (1994) by David Schwartz is a wonderful book which explores large numbers and time. Before reading this delightful book, prepare the children for the vocabulary and mathematical concepts by doing some scaffolding activities.

1. Estimating Time

On the chalkboard, copy two or three questions from the book:

- How long would it take you to count to a million? Record the children's estimates ("Ten minutes"; "One hour"; "All day"; "Never").

- How big would a goldfish bowl have to be to hold one million fish? Ask the children to guess ("Big as this room"; "A big, big, big bowl").

- How tall would a tower made with a million children standing on each other's shoulders be? Invite the children to guess, and record their ideas.

2. Million to Trillion

Tell children that in this book they will be reading the number words *million*, *billion*, and *trillion*. On the chalkboard, write boxes representing the number of letters for each word.

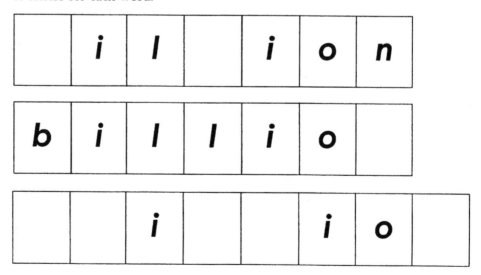

Invite children to help spell the words by asking them to name the sound they hear first, last, and in the middle. Fill in the boxes. This activity will help children anticipate reading these words in context. Ask children to predict which number they will be reading about first.

3. Patterns in Numbers

Write these numbers on the chalkboard:

1

10

100

1,000

10,000

100,000

1,000,000

Ask, "Which number is ten?"; "Which number is a hundred?"; "Can you guess how to write the number for a million?"

This exercise is not intended to teach children how to read large numbers. It is intended to help children notice the pattern in numbers and to use the words *million, billion,* and *trillion.*

4. Read Aloud

Read the book *How Much Is a Million?* Stop after each example for a million. Compare children's predictions with what they have discovered from reading the book. Since the book is patterned, the examples for a billion and a trillion are the same. Ask children to provide a guesstimate for each example.

5. Count to a Million

The author states that it would take 23 days to count to a million. For young children this length of time is difficult to comprehend. For a concrete method of showing them this duration of time, mark the calendar one day at a time for 23 days.

6. A Million Collection

Begin a collection of a million objects—bottle caps, paper clips, toothpicks. (Although the children probably will not achieve this goal, nevertheless it is a good exercise.) Counting may be done in the math center. (To read more about this activity, see *Counting to a Million* on pages 145–146.)

The counting experience will be more valuable if preparations for counting and sorting are made ahead of time. For example, have many containers or plastic bags on hand to store each hundred objects.

Have the children estimate the number of days it will take to reach a million. Have them count the number of days left in the school year. Ask, "Are there enough days to accomplish the task?"

Read other books that deal with large numbers. Some examples are:

One Hundred and One Dalmatians (1990) by Walt Disney, Burbank, CA: Walt Disney Co.

Millions of Cats (1928) by Wanda Gag, New York: Coward-McCann.

Mother Goose Poems about Seasons

1. Read Aloud

Before class, write the following Mother Goose poems, "The Seasons" and "January Brings the Snow," on chart paper. Read the poems.

The Seasons

Spring is showery, flowery, bowery.

Summer is hoppy, croppy, poppy.

Autumn is wheezy, sneezy, freezy.

Winter is slippy, drippy, nippy.

—*Mother Goose*

January Brings the Snow

January brings the snow,

Makes our feet and fingers glow.

February brings the rain,

Thaws the frozen lake again.

March brings breezes loud and shrill,

Stirs the dancing daffodil.

April brings the primrose sweet,

Scatters daisies at our feet.

(Continued on next page)

"January Brings the Snow"—continued

May brings flocks of pretty lambs,

Slipping by their fleecy dams.

June brings tulips, lilies, roses,

Fills the children's hands with posies.

Hot July brings cooling showers,

Apricots, and gillyflowers.

August brings sheaves of corn,

Then the harvest is borne.

Warm September brings the fruit,

Sportsmen then begin to shoot.

Fresh October brings the pheasant,

Then to gather nuts is pleasant.

Dull November brings the blast,

Then the leaves are whirling fast.

Chill December brings the sleet,

Blazing fire, and holiday treat.

—Mother Goose

Ask the children to think about and decide how long a time period each poem talks about. Remind children that one year includes 4 seasons and 12 months. Read the poems again. Count the names of the seasons and the names of the months.

Use a flashlight and globe to demonstrate how the Earth revolves around the sun. Explain that this trip takes one year and produces the different seasons.

After children have had a chance to discuss the poetry, the poems can be used for a variety of language skill demonstrations, such as:

- Capitalization of proper nouns
- Rhyming words
- Blends
- Adjectives

Display both the Mother Goose poems in the reading center for children to read and illustrate or to use in letter- or word-identification activities.

2. Seasonal Words

Tell the children that you are going to reread "January Brings the Snow." Ask them to listen for words they hear in the poem that go with the different seasons. While reading the poem, ask them to indicate these words by raising their hands when they hear a seasonal word.

Across the top of a sheet of chart paper, write the names of the four seasons.

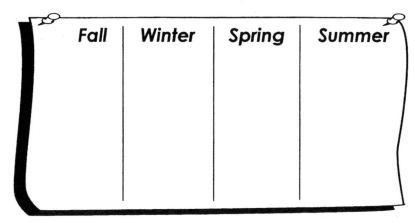

Fall	Winter	Spring	Summer

Begin reading "January Brings the Snow." Stop and ask, "In which season does snow come?" When children answer, "Winter," record the word *snow* under the heading *Winter*. Remind children to listen carefully for seasonal words as you continue to read the poem.

When filling out the seasonal chart, ask children for help with spelling the words. For example, if a student offers the word *hot* to be written under the *Summer* heading, ask the children how to spell *hot*; or write part of the word and ask for the missing letter (h o __).

Mark the first day of fall, winter, spring, and summer on a calendar. Check an almanac for exact dates and times.

Fall, September 21–22

Winter, December 21–22

Spring, March 20–21

Summer, June 20–21

3. Compare/Contrast

In *The Bears' Almanac*, each season is described and seasonal words are listed. Read the section in *The Bears' Almanac* that describes winter. Use a Venn diagram to compare the winter words in that section of the book with the children's list of winter words from the poem, "January Brings the Snow."

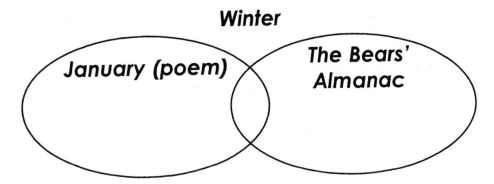

Winter

January (poem)   The Bears' Almanac

4. *Seasons* **Big Book**

   Invite the children to draw or paint pictures to illustrate the poems, "The Seasons" and "January Brings the Snow." Arrange the drawings sequentially, following the seasons. Create a class Big Book with the drawings. Help the children plan which lines from either poem to write on each page. Read this class book many times and make it available in the reading center.

5. **January Snow**

   Distribute a copy of *January Snow* to each child. Have the children complete the missing letters and then read or recite the poem to each other.

6. **Seasons Poem**

   Distribute a copy of *Seasons Poem* to each child for homework. Ask the children to read the poem to a family member and then fill in the missing letters. Provide extra copies of *Seasons Poem* in the writing center.

"The Owl and the Pussy-Cat"

1. Read Aloud

Children love to read and recite the classic poem, "The Owl and the Pussy-Cat" (1935) by Edward Lear. Before class, write the poem (see page 140), "The Owl and the Pussy-Cat," on chart paper.

Read the poem aloud and very dramatically to emphasize the ridiculous plot. Read the poem again. After the two readings, use red and blue markers to circle the character parts of the owl and the pussy-cat. Show children the first set of quotation marks around Owl's words. Tell a child to circle this whole stanza with the red marker. Practice reading this stanza a few times with the whole class. Find the next set of quotation marks around Pussy-Cat's words. Have a child circle this stanza with the blue marker. Read it a few times together. Explain how quotation marks are used to show a spoken phrase or sentence.

The Owl and the Pussy-Cat

The owl and the Pussy-Cat went to sea
In a beautiful pea-green boat.
They took some honey and plenty of money
Wrapped up in a five-pound note.
The owl looked up to the stars above,
And sang to a small guitar,

"Oh, lovely Pussy,
Oh Pussy, my love,
What a beautiful Pussy you are,
You are, you are!
What a beautiful Pussy you are!"

Pussy said to the owl,
"You elegant fowl!
How charmingly sweet you sing!
Oh let us be married;
Too long we have tarried.
But what shall we do for a ring?"

They sailed away for a year and a day,
To the land where the bong-tree grows;
And there in a wood a piggy-wig stood
With a ring at the end of his nose,
His nose, his nose.
With a ring at the end of his nose.

"Dear Pig, are you willing to sell for one shilling
Your ring?" Said the piggy, "I will."
So they took it away and were married the next day
By the turkey who lives on the hill.
They dined on mince and slices of quince,
Which they ate with a runcible spoon.
And hand in hand, on the edge of the sand,
They danced by the light of the moon,
The moon, the moon.
They danced by the light of the moon.

—*Edward Lear*

Display this chart in the drama center so children can take turns reading these two stanzas.

On a chalkboard, write the sentence:

> They sailed away, for a year and a day,
>
> To a land where the bong-tree grows.

Ask children to find out how many days the trip to bong-tree land took.

2. "The Owl and the Pussy-Cat" Sentence Strips

Use "The Owl and the Pussy-Cat" poem for matching activities. Write selected letters, words, and/or whole sentences taken from the text onto 4" x 6" index cards. Show children how to match the letter, word, and/or sentence to the same letter, word, and/or sentence in the text of the poem written on chart paper. Store the letters, words, and sentence cards in large manila envelopes. Rewrite the poem on chart paper. Place the chart paper and envelopes in the reading center.

Alternate Read-Aloud Selections

The Patchwork Quilt (1985) by Valerie Flournoy, New York: Dial Books.

> Grandma has only one year to make a quilt for her granddaughter. This book is beautifully written.

All Year Long (1976) by Richard Scarry, New York: Golden Press.

> This book introduces time, days of the week, months, and seasons.

The Snow Speaks (1992) by Nancy White Carlstrom, Boston: Little, Brown.

> Children discover the many signs of winter in this book.

Arthur's April Fool (1983) by Marc Brown, Boston: Little, Brown.

> This book is one in a series that deals with Arthur's funny antics. It is a favorite of young readers.

Bringing the Rain to Kapiti Plain (1981) by Verna Aardema, New York: Dial Press.

> This authentically and beautifully illustrated book set in Africa speaks to the patterns of life. The format of this tale resembles that of *The House That Jack Built*.

Songs, Movement, and Games

Movement

1. Class Rhythm Band

Collect instruments for a rhythm band. As mentioned earlier, keeping rhythm helps develop children's understanding of time. You'll need several of each, so that every child has an instrument:

Tambourines	Sticks	Bells
Triangles	Drums	Blocks

Using *Instrument Symbols* (see page 151), create a set of practice symbol cards (i.e., a set of one of each instrument).

Give each child an instrument. Seat the children with the same instruments close to each other. Demonstrate how to play each instrument correctly.

Using the practice symbol cards, show a card and have the children holding that instrument play while the other children remain silent.

Using *Instrument Symbols*, develop another set of cards. This time, create large cards that show children which instruments to play and how many times they should play their instruments. Practice playing the music a few times.

Invite children to create their own musical arrangements and record them on chart paper for other children to play. One or two children's arrangements could be incorporated into the activities for the Good Times Parade. Have *Instrument Symbols* available in the discovery center for children to cut and paste together to create original musical arrangements.

Songs

1. Patriotic Songs

Have children practice singing songs that celebrate their country. For instance, some of the patriotic songs for the United States are "The Star Spangled Banner," "America the Beautiful," "You're a Grand Old Flag," and "God Bless America." Help children use instruments to keep time as they sing.

Learning Centers

Drama Center

1. "The Owl and the Pussy-Cat"

"The Owl and the Pussy-Cat" is an excellent poem/story for dramatizing. Have available scarves, a long flowing skirt, and dress shoes to help children act more dramatically. Have available the *Owl* and the *Pussy-Cat Masks* (see pages 152–153). Tell children to color, cut out, and glue the masks to a paper plate; then cut out eyes and attach a popsicle stick as a handle to hold the mask. Display "The Owl and the Pussy-Cat" poem created earlier (see pages 139–140). Have children take turns reading the stanzas.

2. Dialogue Strips

Prepare sentence strips with the dialogue of each character in "The Owl and the Pussy-Cat" poem. Have available the *Owl* and the *Pussy-Cat Masks*.

Tell children in the center to work together to sequence the sentence strips in the correct order, then wear the face masks to read and act out the dialogue.

Writing Center

1. *ABC Book of Special Days*

Instruct children to draw or cut out magazine pictures or add photos to the *ABC Book of Special Days* created earlier (see page 129). Display a variety of alphabet books for inspiration and guidance.

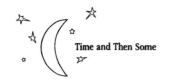
2. Favorite Days

Have paper available for creating books. Tell children to write their own books about their favorite days of the year.

3. Good Times Parade Invitations

Children can create the invitations to attend the Good Times Parade. The invitations can be sent home and to other classes.

Reading Center

1. *Seasons* Big Book

Display the *Seasons* Big Book created earlier (see page 139) for children to read.

2. Rhyming Words

Display "The Owl and the Pussy-Cat" poem and have available envelopes with sentence strips created earlier (see page 141). Challenge children to read the poem "The Owl and the Pussy-Cat" and to try the matching activity. Then list all the rhyming pairs they can find in the poem.

3. Mother Goose Poems

Display the chart of Mother Goose poems created earlier (see page 136–137). Invite children to illustrate the poems and practice letter and word identification as they read them.

4. Cookbook Fun

Collect copies of cookbooks written especially for young children. Ask children to read the books and find recipes that might be served to the guests for the Good Times Parade celebration. If a recipe is selected, ask children to make a grocery list for ingredients needed to make the recipe.

5. Holiday Lists

Display the *Special Days* chart created earlier (see pages 128–129). Have available extra copies of *My Special Days* (see page 148) and invite the children to continue to work on categorizing the charted list.

6. "The Owl and the Pussy-Cat" Sentence Strips

Write each line of "The Owl and the Pussy-Cat" on sentence strips cut in half (3" x 8½"). Cut apart the lines of the poem. Store these sentence strips in a pocket folder. Have children assemble the poem, using the sentence strips. When they are finished they could check their work against the charted poem.

Math Center

1. Counting Days

Reproduce a calendar or have several calendars available in the center. On large chart paper, write the following questions and others like them. Create three columns, as shown in the illustration.

How many days are there from:	Number of days	Agree	Disagree
The first day of school until Halloween			
Valentine's Day until President's Day			
St. Patrick's Day until the first day of spring			

For this activity, center participants should work together as a small group. Referring to the calendar, have one child count the days between the events, then record that number in the first column, initialing the entry. Have another child (and other children who do this activity) also count the number of days, and either initial the second column or enter another number in the third column, depending on whether the child agrees or disagrees with the first child's count. When children disagree, have them recount. This is a wonderful activity for demonstrating the value of checking one's work.

To help children keep track of counting, suggest that they put a bean, paper clip, penny, or other small object on each square that represents a day.

2. Counting to a Million

Have the children decide on a small object which they would like to collect (e.g., plastic bottle caps or tabs from aluminum cans). Challenge the children to bring in one million bottle caps and provide a large box for the collection. When there are a significant number of caps, demonstrate how children can count by 10s, and that 10 x 10 = 100 bottle caps. The children put 100 caps into a plastic bag and label the bag with the number 100. When there are 10 plastic bags, show the children that now they have 1,000 bottle caps.

Expect the children to tire of this project long before they can collect 1,000,000 caps. However, they will have had many valuable counting experiences.

Certainly they will appreciate that 1,000 is a large number and that 1,000,000 is a huge number.

Discovery Center

1. Time Diagrams

Have a globe and flashlight available for student exploration. Suggest that children draw diagrams to demonstrate day and night, the lunar month, and the Earth's trip around the sun. Encourage the children to explain their diagrams to the rest of the class.

2. Musical Arrangements

Have available copies of *Instrument Symbols* (see page 151) for children to cut and paste to create original music. Children can experiment playing various band instruments. Encourage children to create compositions for the Good Times Parade.

3. Collections

Challenge the children to:

- Find coins that were minted in their birth years
- Collect commemoration coins
- Begin a stamp collection by year of issue

4. Growth Rings

Bring in a large branch of a tree which recently fell off or was cut off. Show the annual rings to the children. Have the children count rings to find out the age of the tree. Mark each ring with a pin and have the children research at least one important event that occurred during each year.

Art Center

1. Favorite Holiday

Provide mural paper and watercolor paints. Have the children paint scenes of their favorite holiday, special days in the year, or good times on the mural paper. Encourage them to paint smaller pictures representing the various seasons, holidays, or special days.

2. Good Times Parade Posters

Have the children make posters or banners advertising the Good Times Parade.

3. Good Times Parade Costumes

Collect and have materials available to help children prepare their costumes for the Good Times Parade. Decorated paper bags make great costumes.

Sand and Water Center

1. Pastimes

Have children bring toy boats to play with at the water table or in a large pan of water. The boat activity will stimulate good memories and discussions about annual events such as beach trips, family vacations, and fishing adventures. Have children describe how long ago the experiences occurred using one of the terms: *day, week, month,* or *year.*

Cooking Experience

Cooking Through the Year

Give each child a copy of *Cooking Through the Year* (see page 154) to take home and talk about with an adult. When all children have brought their recipes, talk about the months and the representative foods. Have the children compile a class cookbook, organizing the recipes by month. Help them choose a title for the cookbook. Encourage them to draw illustrations for the recipes. Make copies of the cookbook and present them to parents and other guests during the Good Times Parade celebration.

Name _____ **Date** _____

My Special Days

My Favorite Days	Dates
1.	
2.	
3.	
4.	
5.	
Days My Family Celebrates	**Dates**
1.	
2.	
3.	
4.	
5.	
Days My Country Celebrates	**Dates**
1.	
2.	
3.	
4.	
5.	

Name _____ Date _____

 **January Snow**

Add the missing letters. Draw some pictures too, if you want.

January brings the __ __ ow,

Makes our feet and fingers __ __ __ w.

February brings the rai __ .

Thaws the frozen lakes agai __ .

March brings breezes loud and shri __ __ .

Stirs the dancing daffodi __ .

April brings the primrose sw __ __ __ .

Scatters daisies at our f __ __ __ .

Name _____ **Date** _____

Seasons Poem

1. Read this Mother Goose poem with someone.

> ### The Seasons
>
> **Spring is showery, flowery, bowery.**
>
> **Summer is hoppy, croppy, poppy.**
>
> **Autumn is wheezy, sneezy, freezy.**
>
> **Winter is slippy, drippy, nippy.**

----

2. Fold this page along the dotted line. Turn back the folded part of the page so you can't see the poem. Fill in the missing letters on the poem below. When you are finished, unfold the page and check your work.

> ### The Seasons
>
> __ __ ring is showery, flowery, bowery.
>
> __ ummer __ __ hoppy, croppy, poppy.
>
> Autumn is wheez __ , sneez __ , freez__ .
>
> __ inter is __ __ ippy, __ __ ippy, __ ippy.

3. Invent a poem by writing different consonant blends on the lines. Read your new poem to someone.

> ### My Seasons
>
> Spring is __ __ owery, __ __ wery, __ __ wery.
>
> Summer is __ __ oppy, __ __ oppy, __ __ oppy.
>
> Autumn is __ __ eezy, __ __ eezy, __ __ eezy.
>
> Winter is __ __ ippy, __ __ ippy, __ __ ippy.

Some blends you could use:

sp   sl   br   tr   bl   cl   sw   gr   sn   gl   fl   st   pr

Instrument Symbols

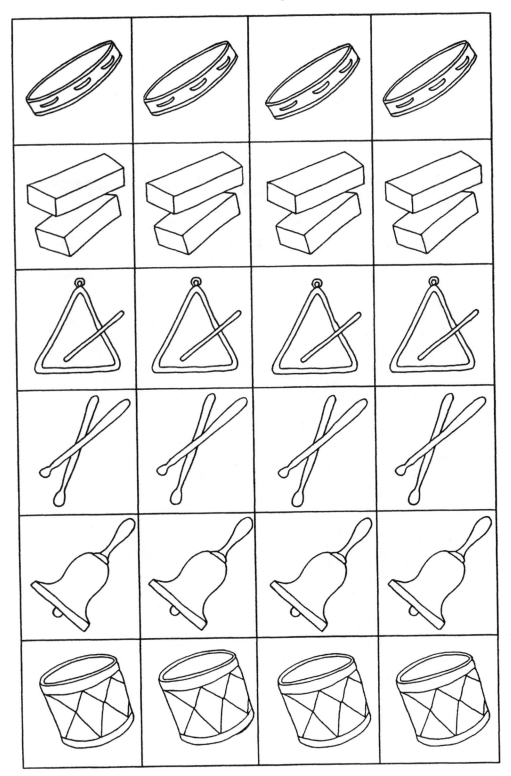

Owl Mask

Pussy-Cat Mask

Name _____ **Date** _____

Cooking Through the Year

Choose your favorite month. Bring to school one or two recipes for the food listed next to that month. We will be creating a class cookbook of recipes.

Month	Food	Some Examples of Recipes
September	apples	Apple Fritters
October	pumpkins	Baked Pumpkin Seeds
November	sweet potatoes	Sweet Potato Spoon Bread
December	candy	Fudge
January	ice cream	Ice-Cream Cone Clowns
February	pudding	Flan
March	bread	Bagels
April	eggs	Deviled Eggs
May	cookies	Hamentash
June	strawberries	Strawberry Shortcake
July	corn	Green Corn Tamales
August	peaches	Peach Cobbler

Appendices

Name _____ **Date** _____

My Week in Centers

Mark the face that shows how you felt during center time.

On Monday, I went to _____ . ☺ ☺ ☹

and _____ . ☺ ☺ ☹

On Tuesday, I went to _____ . ☺ ☺ ☹

and _____ . ☺ ☺ ☹

On Wednesday, I went to _____ . ☺ ☺ ☹

and _____ . ☺ ☺ ☹

On Thursday, I went to _____ . ☺ ☺ ☹

and _____ . ☺ ☺ ☹

On Friday, I went to _____ . ☺ ☺ ☹

and _____ . ☺ ☺ ☹

The best thing I did this week was...

_____

_____

_____

_____

_____

Time and Then Some

Draw one thing you did.

I wish…

_____

- -

_____

_____

- -

_____

Tell more if you want.

- -

_____

_____

- -

_____

Educator comments:

Learning Behaviors Checklist

Name _____

Date _____

Key

NY = Not Yet
IP = In Process
PR = Proficient

	NY	IP	PR
The student actively participates in class activities.			
The student chooses manipulatives for exploration and invention.			
The student solves problems creatively.			
The student completes assigned tasks.			
The student makes good choices in centers.			
The student works cooperatively in a small group.			
The student works cooperatively with peers.			
The student is sensitive to others' needs.			
The student helps organize and maintain the classroom.			
The student accepts constructive criticism.			
The student sees mistakes as a positive learning experience.			
The student is curious about the unknown.			
The student is self-motivated.			
The student sorts by:			
Size			
Color			
Other attributes			

Comments:

Listening Checklist

Name _____

Key

NY = Not Yet
IP = In Process
PR = Proficient

Date _____

	NY	IP	PR
The student listens attentively to peers.			
The student makes eye-to-eye contact with the speaker.*			
The student listens with interested expressions.			
The student turns body toward the speaker.			
The student listens to and follows:			
One direction			
Two directions			
Two or more directions			
The student attends to:			
One-to-one conversations			
A story			
Class discussions			

* Respect cultural differences with regard to adult-child eye contact.

Comments:

Speaking Checklist

Name _____

Date _____

	NY	IP	PR
The student contributes to classroom discussions.			
The student shares knowledge and information with classmates.			
The student asks questions to clarify meaning.			
The student uses expressive language to:			
Express ideas			
Compare and contrast			
Sequence events			
Name common objects			
Distinguish important from unimportant information			
Articulate personal plans			
Relate personal experiences			
Identify details of a picture			
In conversation, the student:			
Initiates topics			
Waits to share			
Disagrees without disrupting			
Asks for clarification			
Elaborates on a topic			
Responds appropriately			
Stays on topic			
The student correctly articulates:			
Sounds			
Words			
The student uses the words *more, less, the same* when describing graph data.			

Comments:

Reading Checklist

Name _____

Date _____

Key

NY = Not Yet
IP = In Process
PR = Proficient

	NY	IP	PR
The student holds book appropriately.			
The student turns pages correctly.			
The student demonstrates interest in and love for reading.			
The student relates literature to real life.			
The student chooses to read books independently.			
The student recognizes sound/symbol relationships.			
The student chooses to read when given a choice.			
The student displays confidence as a reader.			
The student has favorite books.			
The student elaborates on a book.			
The student makes predictions about what will happen in the story.			
The student remembers pictures and text to support and clarify ideas.			
The student retells a story with:			
A beginning and ending			
Main points in sequence			
Details			
The student understands real versus fiction.			
The student shares insights gained by reading.			
The student talks meaningfully about:			
Characters			
Setting			
Problem			
Solution			
Tension			

Comments:

Writing Checklist

Name _____

Date _____

	NY	IP	PR
The student demonstrates interest in writing.			
The student makes connections from reading to own writing.			
The student writes own name.			
The student recognizes punctuation:			
Period			
Question mark			
Exclamation point			
Quotation marks			
The student is making progress toward conventional writing through:			
Pictures			
Scribbles			
Random letters			
Labeling (words)			
Correct form for a letter			
Sound-letter correspondence:			
Correct initial consonants			
Final consonants			
Blends			
Word endings			
Spaces between words			
Sentences			
Punctuated text			
Capitalization			
Some conventional spellings			
The student enjoys writing and authoring books.			
The student is writing text that demonstrates appropriate:			
Length			
Descriptive vocabulary			

Comments:

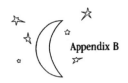
Award-Winning Books

The Caldecott Medal

The Caldecott Medal is awarded annually by The Association for Library Service to Children. In 1938, the first Caldecott Medal, donated by Frederic G. Melcher (1879–1963), was awarded to the artist of the most distinguished American picture book for children published in the United States during the preceding year. The name of Randolph Caldecott, the famous English illustrator of books for children, was chosen for the medal because his work best represented the "joyousness of picture books as well as their beauty."

The Caldecott Medal Books (Including Names of Illustrators)

1998 *Rapunzel*. Paul Zelinsky.

1997 *Golem*. David Wisniewski.

1996 *Officer Buckle & Gloria*. Peggy Rathmann.

1995 *Smoky Night*. Eve Bunting. (Ill. by David Diaz.)

1994 *Grandfather's Journey*. Allen Say.

1993 *Mirette on the Highwire*. Emily Arnold McCully.

1992 *Tuesday*. David Wiesner.

1991 *Black and White*. David Macaulay.

1990 *Lon Po Po: A Red Riding Hood Story from China*. Ed Young.

1989 *Song and Dance Man*. Karen Ackerman. (Ill. by Stephen Gammel.)

1988 *Owl Moon*. Jane Yolen. (Ill. by John Schoenherr.)

1987 *Hey, Al*. Arthur Yorinks. (Ill. by Richard Egielski.)

1986 *The Polar Express*. Chris Van Allsburg.

1985 *Saint George and the Dragon*. Margaret Hodges. (Ill. by Trina Schart Hyman.)

1984 *The Glorious Flight: Across the Channel with Louis Bleriot*. Alice and Martin Provensen.

1983 *Shadow*. Blaise Cendars. (Ill. by Marcia Brown.)

1982 *Jumanji*. Chris Van Allsburg.

1981 *Fables*. Arnold Lobel.

1980 *Ox-Cart Man*. Donald Hall (Ill. by Barbara Cooney.)

1979 *The Girl Who Loved Wild Horses*. Paul Goble.

1978 *Noah's Ark*. Peter Spier.

1977 *Ashanti to Zulu: African Traditions*. Margaret Musgrove. (Ill. by Leo and Diane Dillon.)

1976 *Why Mosquitoes Buzz in People's Ears*. Verna Aardema. (Ill. by Leo and Diane Dillon.)

1975 *Arrow to the Sun*. Gerald McDermott.

1974 *Duffy and the Devil*. Harve Zemach. (Ill. by Margot Zemach.)

1973 *The Funny Little Woman*. Arlene Mosel. (Ill. by Blair Lent.)

1972 *One Fine Day*. Nonny Hogrogian.

1971 *A Story A Story*. Gail E. Haley.

1970 *Sylvester and the Magic Pebble*. William Steig.

1969 *The Fool of the World and the Flying Ship*. Arthur Ransome. (Ill. by Uri Schulevitz.)

1968 *Drummer Hoff*. Barbara Emberley. (Ill. by Ed Emberley.)

1967 *Sam, Bangs & Moonshine*. Evaline Ness.

1966 *Always Room for One More*. Sorche Nic Leodhas. (Ill. by Nonny Hogrogian.)

1965 *May I Bring a Friend?* Beatrice Schenk de Regnier.

1964 *Where the Wild Things Are*. Maurice Sendak.

1963 *The Snowy Day*. Ezra Jack Keats.

1962 *Once a Mouse*. Maricia Brown.

1961 *Baboushka and the Three Kings*. Ruth Robbins. (Ill. by Nicholas Sidjakov.)

1960 *Nine Days to Christmas*. Marie Hall Ets. (Ill. by Marie Hall Ets.)

1959 *Chanticleer and the Fox*. Geoffrey Chaucer. (Ill. by Barbara Cooney.)

1958 *Time of Wonder*. Robert McCloskey.

1957 *A Tree Is Nice*. Janice Udry.

1956 *Frog Went A-Courtin'*. John Langstaff. (Ill. by Feodor Rojankovsky.)

1955 *Cinderella*. Marcia Brown.

1954 *Madeline's Rescue*. Ludwig Bemelmans.

1953 *The Biggest Bear*. Lynd Ward.

1952 *Finders Keepers*. Will Lipkind.

1951 *The Egg Tree*. Katherine Milhous.

1950 *Song of the Swallows*. Leo Politi.

1949 *The Big Snow*. Berta and Elmer Hader.

1948 *White Snow, Bright Snow*. Alvin Tresselt. (Ill. by Roger Duvoisin.)

1947 *The Little Island*. Margaret Wise Brown. (Ill. by Leonard Weisgard.)

1946 *The Rooster Crows*. Maude and Miska Petersham.

1945 *Prayer for a Child*. Rachel Field. (Ill. by Elizabeth Orton Jones.)

1944 *Many Moons*. James Thurber. (Ill. by Louis Slobodkin.)

1943 *The Little House*. Virginia Lee Burton.

1942 *Make Way for Ducklings*. Robert McCloskey.

1941 *They Were Strong and Good*. Robert Lawson.

1940 *Abraham Lincoln*. Ingri and Edgar Parin d'Aulaire.

1939 *Mei Li*. Thomas Handforth.

1938 *Animals of the Bible*. Helen Dean Fish. (Ill. by Dorothy Lathrop.)

The Newbery Medal

The Newbery Medal was first presented in 1922 to the author of the most distinguished book written for children in the preceding year. The award was named for John Newbery, who published, printed, and sold books for children during the 18th century in England.

The Newbery Medal Books (Including Names of Authors)

1998 *Out of the Dust*. Karen Hesse.

1997 *The View from Saturday*. E.L. Konigsburg.

1996 *The Midwife's Apprentice*. Karen Cushman.

1995 *Walk Two Moons*. Sharon Creech.

1994 *The Giver*. Lois Lowry.

1993 *Missing May*. Cynthia Rylant.

1992 *Shiloh*. Phyllis Reynolds Naylor.

1991 *Maniac McGee*. Jerry Spinelli.

1990 *Number the Stars*. Lois Lowry.

1989 *Joyful Noises: Poems for Two Voices*. Paul Fleischman.

1988 *Lincoln: A Photobiography*. Russell Freedman.

1987 *Whipping Boy*. Sid Fleischman.

1986 *Sarah Plain and Tall*. Patricia MacLachlan.

1985 *The Hero and the Crown*. Robin McKinley.

1984 *Dear Mr. Henshaw*. Beverly Cleary.

1983 *Dicey's Song*. Cynthia Voigt.

1982 *A Visit to William Blake's Inn: Poems for Innocent and Experienced Travelers*. Nancy Willard.

1981 *Jacob Have I Loved*. Katherine Paterson.

1980 *A Gathering of Days: A New England Girl's Journal*. Joan W. Blos.

1979 *The Westing Game*. Ellen Raskin.

1978 *Bridge to Terabithia*. Katherine Paterson.

1977 *Roll of Thunder, Hear My Cry*. Mildred D. Taylor.

1976 *The Grey King*. Susan Cooper.

1975 *M. C. Higgins the Great*. Virginia Hamilton.

1974 *The Slave Dancer*. Paula Fox.

1973 *Julie of the Wolves*. Jean C. George.

1972 *Mrs. Frisby and the Rats of NIMH*. Robert C. O'Brien.

1971 *Summer of the Swans*. Betsy Byars.

1970 *Sounder*. William H. Armstrong.

1969 *The High King*. Lloyd Alexander.

1968 *From the Mixed-Up Files of Mrs. Basil E. Frankweiler*. E. L. Konigsburg.

1967 *Up a Road Slowly*. Irene Hunt.

1966 *I, Juan de Pareja*. Elizabeth Borton de Trevino.

1965 *Shadow of a Bull*. Maia Wojciechowska.

1964 *It's Like This, Cat*. Emily C. Neville.

1963 *A Wrinkle in Time*. Madeleine L'Engle.

1962 *The Bronze Bow*. Elizabeth G. Speare.

1961 *Island of the Blue Dolphins*. Scott O'Dell.

1960 *Onion John*. Joseph Krumgold.

1959 *The Witch of Blackbird Pond*. Elizabeth G. Speare.

1958 *Rifles for Watie*. Harold V. Keith.

1957 *Miracles on Maple Hill*. Virginia Sorensen.

1956 *Carry On, Mr. Bowditch*. Jean Lee Latham.

1955 *The Wheel on the School*. Meindert Dejong.

1954 *...And Now Miguel*. Joseph Krumgold.

1953 *Secret of the Andes*. Ann Nolan Clark.

1952 *Ginger Pye*. Eleanor Estes.

1951 *Amos Fortune, Free Man*. Elizabeth Yates.

1950 *The Door in the Wall*. Marguerite de Angeli.

1949 *King of the Wind*. Marguerite Henry.

1948 *The Twenty-One Balloons*. William Pene du Bois.

1947 *Miss Hickory*. Carolyn S. Bailey.

1946 *Strawberry Girl*. Lois Lenski.

1945 *Rabbit Hill*. Robert Lawson.

1944 *Johnny Tremain*. Esther Forbes.

1943 *Adam of the Road*. Elizabeth Janet Gray.

1942 *The Matchlock Gun*. Walter D. Edmonds.

1941 *Call It Courage*. Armstrong Sperry.

1940 *Daniel Boone*. James Daugherty.

1939 *Thimble Summer*. Elizabeth Enright.

1938 *The White Stag*. Kate Seredy.

1937 *Roller Skates*. Ruth Sawyer.

1936 *Caddie Woodlawn*. Carol Ryrie Brink.

1935 *Dobry*. Monica Shannon.

1934 *Invincible Louisa*. Cornelia Meigs.

1933 *Yung Fu of the Upper Yangtze*. Elizabeth Lewis.

1932 *Waterless Mountain*. Laura Armer.

1931 *The Cat Who Went to Heaven*. Elizabeth Coatsworth.

1930 *Hitty, Her First Hundred Years*. Rachel Field.

1929 *The Trumpeter of Krakow*. Eric P. Kelly.

1928 *Gay Neck, The Story of a Pigeon*. Dhan Mukerji.

1927 *Smoky, The Cowhorse*. Will James.

1926 *Shen of the Sea*. Arthur Chrisman.

1925 *Tales from Silver Lands*. Charles Finger.

1924 *The Dark Frigate*. Charles Hawes.

1923 *The Voyages of Dr. Doolittle*. Hugh Lofting.

1922 *The Story of Mankind*. Henrik Van Loon.

The Coretta Scott King Award

The Coretta Scott King Award commemorates the life and work of Dr. Martin Luther King, Jr., and his wife, Coretta Scott King. Since 1970, the award is annually given to a black author, and, since 1974, to a black illustrator whose works are considered "outstanding, inspirational, and educational contributions to literature for children and young people." On the medal are the words *peace, brotherhood, non-violent social change*.

Coretta Scott King Award Books

1998 *Forged by Fire*. Sharon Draper (author).

In Daddy's Arms I Am Tall. Javaka Steptoe (illustrator).

1997 *Slam!* Walter Dean Myers (author).

Minty: A Story of Young Harriet Tubman. Jerry Pinkney (illustrator).

1996 *Her Stories: African American Folktales, Fairy Tales and True Tales*. Virginia Hamilton (author).

The Middle Passage: White Ships Black Cargo. Tom Feelings (illustrator).

1995 *Christmas in the Big House, Christmas in the Quarters*. Patricia C. and Fredrick L. McKissack (authors).

The Creation. James E. Ransome (illustrator).

1994 *Toning the Sweep*. Angela Johnson (author).

Soul Looks Back in Wonder. Tom Feelings (illustrator).

1993 *The Dark-Thirty: Southern Tales of the Supernatural*. Patricia C. McKissack (author).

The Origin of Life on Earth: An African Creation Myth. Kathleen Atkins Wilson (illustrator).

1992 *Now Is Your Time! The African American Struggle for Freedom*. Walter Dean Myers (author).

Tar Beach. Faith Ringgold (illustrator).

1991 *The Road to Memphis*. Mildred D. Taylor (author).

Aïda. Leo and Diane Dillon (illustrators).

1990 *A Long Hard Journey: The Story of the Pullman Porter*. Patricia C. and Fredrick L. McKissack (authors).

Nathaniel Talking. Jan Spivey Gilchrist (illustrator).

1989 *Fallen Angels*. Walter Dean Myers (author).

Mirandy and Brother Wind. Jerry Pinkney (illustrator).

1988 *The Friendship*. Mildred D. Taylor (author).

Mufaro's Beautiful Daughters: An African Tale. John Steptoe (illustrator).

1987 *Justin and the Best Biscuits in the World*. Mildred Pitts Walter (author).

Half a Moon and One Whole Star. Jerry Pinkney (illustrator).

1986 *The People Could Fly: American Black Folktales*. Virginia Hamilton (author).

The Patchwork Quilt. Jerry Pinkney (illustrator).

1985 *Motown and Didi: A Love Story*. Walter Dean Myers (author).

1984 *Everett Anderson's Goodbye*. Lucille Clifton (author).

My Mama Needs Me. Pat Cummings (illustrator).

1983 *Sweet Whispers, Brother Rush*. Virginia Hamilton (author).

Black Child. Peter Magubane (illustrator).

1982 *Let the Circle Be Unbroken*. Mildred D. Taylor (author).

Mama Crocodile: An Uncle Amadou Tale from Senegal. John Steptoe (illustrator).

1981 *This Life*. Sidney Poitier (author).

Beat the Story Drum, Pum-Pum. Ashley Bryan (illustrator).

1980 *The Young Landlords*. Walter Dean Myers (author).

Cornrows. Carole Byard (illustrator).

1979 *Escape to Freedom: A Play about Young Frederick Douglass*. Ossie Davis (author).

Something on My Mind. Tom Feelings (illustrator).

1978 *Africa Dream*. Eloise Greenfield (author).

1977 *The Story of Stevie Wonder*. James Haskins (author).

1976 *Duey's Tale*. Pearl Bailey (author).

1975 *The Legend of Africania*. Dorothy Robinson (author).

1974 *Ray Charles*. Sharon Bell Mathis (author).

    Ray Charles. George Ford (illustrator).

1973 *I Never Had It Made: The Autobiography of Jackie Robinson*. (as told to) Alfred Duckett (author).

1972 *17 Black Artists*. Elton C. Fax (author).

1971 *Black Troubadour: Langston Hughes*. Charlemae Rollins (author).

1970 *Martin Luther King, Jr.: Man of Peace*. Lillie Patterson (author).

References

Anderson, L. (1950). *The syncopated clock* [Musical score]. Miami, FL: CPP/Belwin.

Bang, M. (1989). *Ten, nine, eight.* Toronto, Canada: Scholastic.

Barrett, J. (1992). *Benjamin's 365 birthdays.* New York: Atheneum.

Bruner, J.S. (1975). The ontogenesis of speech acts. *Journal of Child Language, 2,* 1–40.

Calkins, L. (1986). *The art of teaching writing.* Portsmouth, NH: Heinemann.

Cambourne, B., and Turbill, J. (1987). *Coping with chaos.* Portsmouth, NH: Heinemann.

Carl, E. (1983). *The very hungry caterpillar.* New York: Philomel.

Carlstrom, N.W. (1986). *Jesse bear, what will you wear?* New York: Macmillan.

Cazden, C.B. (1992). *Whole language plus.* New York: Teacher's College Press.

Dewey, J. (1897). *My pedagogic creed.* New York: Kellogg.

Eggleton, J. (1988). Please, Mr. Clock. In *Now we are six,* Bothell, WA: The Wright Group.

Elkind, D. (1986). Formal education and early childhood education: An essential difference. *Phi Delta Kappan, 67,* 631–636.

Goodman, K. (1986). *What's whole in whole language?* Portsmouth, NH: Heinemann.

Graves, M., Graves, B., and Braaten, S. (1996). Scaffolded reading experiences for inclusive classes. *Educational Leadership, 53*(5), 14–16.

Harp, B. (1991). *Assessment in whole language programs and evaluation.* Norwood, MA: Christopher Gordon.

Harste, J., Short, K., and Burke, C. (1988). *Creating classrooms for authors.* Portsmouth, NH: Heinemann.

Herman, J., Aschbacher, P., and Winters, L. (1992). *A practical guide to alternative assessment*. Alexandria, VA: Association for Supervision and Curriculum Development.

Holdaway, D. (1979). *The foundations of literacy*. Portsmouth, NH: Heinemann.

Katz, L. (1987) Early education: What should young children be doing? In S. Kagan and E. Zigler (Eds.), *Early schooling: A national debate* (pp. 151–165). New Haven: Yale University Press.

Lombardino, L., Bedford, T., Fortier, C., Carter, J., Brandi, J., (1997). Invented spelling: Developmental patterns in kindergarten children and guidelines for early literacy intervention. *Language, Speech, and Hearing Services in Schools, 28*, 333–343.

McTighe, J. (1996/1997). What happens between assessments. *Educational Leadership, 54*(4), 6–12.

Meisels, S. (1996/1997). Using work sampling in authentic assessments. *Educational Leadership, 54*(4), 60–65.

Mirenda, P. (1993). Bonding the uncertain mosaic. *Augmentative and Alternative Communication, 9*, 3–9.

Montgomery, J. (1996, April). *Learning words to use: Using words to learn*. Presentation at the annual convention of the Texas Speech-Language-Hearing Association, Dallas, Texas.

Parish, M. (1950). *The syncopated clock* [Lyrics]. Miami, FL: CPP/Belwin.

Pearson, P.D. (1996). Reclaiming the center. In M.F. Graves, P. van den Broek, and B.M. Taylor (Eds.), *The first r: A right of all children* (pp. 259–274), New York: Teacher's College Press.

Piaget, J., and Inhelder, B. (1969). *The psychology of the child*. New York: Basic.

Rosenshine, B., and Meister, C. (1992). The use of scaffolds for teaching higher-level cognitive strategies. *Educational Leadership, 49*(7), 26–33.

Scherer, M.M. (Ed.). (1996/1997). Teaching for authentic student performance [Entire issue]. *Educational Leadership, 54*(4).

Schwartz, D. (1994). *How much is a million?* New York: Mulberry Books.

Seefeldt, C. (1988). Appropriate and cognitive curriculum in the kindergarten. In *New trends in kindergarten programming: A mini conference* (pp. 60–64). Alexandria, VA: Association for Supervision and Curriculum Development.

Staton, J. (1984). Thinking together: Interaction in children's reasoning. In C. Thais and C. Suhor (Eds.), *Speaking and writing* (pp. 144–187). Urbana, IL: National Council of Teachers of English.

Strickland, D., and Morrow, L. M. (Eds.). (1989). *Emerging literacy: Young children learn to read and write.* Newark, DE: International Reading Association.

Sweet, A.P. (1993). *State of the art: Transforming ideas for teaching and learning to read.* Washington, DC: U.S. Department of Education.

Tobalsky, S. (1998). *My Week.* Unpublished poem.

Thais, C. (1986). *Language across the curriculum in the elementary grades.* Urbana, IL: Educational Resources Information Center (ERIC).

Tierney, R., Carter, M., and Desai, R. (1991). *Portfolio assessment in the reading-writing classroom.* Norwood, MA: Christopher Gordon.

Tortoriello, T. (1992). *9:00 o'clock for you!* Unpublished poem.

Ward, C. (1988). *Cookie's week.* New York: Putnam.

Vygotsky, L.S. (1978). *Mind in society: The development of higher psychological processes.* Cambridge: Harvard University Press.